the
RAINBOW
years

the RAINBOW years

the **pluses** of being **50+**

Barrie Hopson and **Mike Scally**

Middlesex
University
PRESS

First published in 2008 by Middlesex University Press

Copyright © Barrie Hopson and Mike Scally

ISBN 978 1 904750 59 8

A CIP catalogue record for this book is available from
The British Library

Design by Helen Taylor

Printed in the UK by Ashford Colour Press

Middlesex University Press
Tel: +44 (0)20 8411 4162
Fax: +44 (0)20 8411 4167

www.mupress.co.uk

Praise for *The Rainbow Years*...

"Hopson and Scally have done it again. The Rainbow Years is an indispensable toolkit for the baby boomer generation."

John Cull
Mentoring Consultant, PRIME (Prince's Initiative for Mature Enterprise)

"A rich resource for those preparing for their third age, and for workshops designed to help them – replete with thought jumps and 'Aha' moments."

Professor Tony Watts
Founding Fellow and Life President, National Institute for Careers Education and Counselling

"The Rainbow Years *provides more than an inspiring philosophy. It provides practical tools that people can use to shape their future lives. People often go through three stages in life: simplicity, complexity and simplicity. The second simplicity is a profound simplicity, however, because it is coloured by life experience. The* Rainbow Years *embodies this wisdom. It provides a treasure chest of knowledge that people can use to live fulfilling lives."*

Mike Pegg
Managing Director, The Strengths Academy

"The Rainbow Years: the pluses of being 50+ offers an insightful and challenging review of seven life themes that affect those of us who are in the second half of our lives. It is a refreshingly optimistic and provocative book. Readers can dip into the content as the mood takes them and draw on some of the 48 diagnostic questionnaires and other activities that have been designed to help us get the most out of life. Highly recommended for those with an enquiring mind."

Professor John Hayes
Leeds University Business School

"The Rainbow Years is another great resource for the over 50s. Having recently launched our new website www.fiftyforward.co.uk we recognise how much this audience values practical advice and guidance on all aspects of life in a fun and interactive format."

Kirstie Donnelly
Director of Products and Marketing, learndirect

"The Rainbow Years provides a valuable resource to deal with and plan for change in the second phase of the journey in one's working life. Comprising information, planner, map and compass, it will date slowly, like those that use it."

Dr John Papworth-Smith
Occupational Medical Officer, Occupational Health Service, University of Leeds

"Fans of Build Your Own Rainbow *won't be disappointed! The Rainbow Years builds upon the same underpinning philosophical foundations, and the sections on the impact of events in our lives and transitions are especially thought provoking and enlightening. Helpful to readers and 'advisers' alike, I commend this excellent toolkit to all looking for confirmation that life beyond 50 is full of opportunity and fun."*

Paul Chubb
Non-executive Director and Policy Adviser, Careers England

Acknowledgements

Authors must be the most blessed of creatures. Everyday, the world most generously gifts to their eyes and ears a trove of characters, contacts, contexts, cameos, insights, episodes and experiences that are hugely valuable stimuli and inspirations. The writer's role is to observe, absorb, reflect, filter, draw learning, find links, spot themes and search for some alchemy to add to the common good. In this book our quest has been to learn from many people who are living out the second half of their lives in unique, remarkable, creative, adventurous, meaningful and admirable ways and to make the structure of their magic available to more of us. Given that the 50+ generation has opportunities never before available to this age group, how can we make our extra decades enriching, rewarding, healthier and happier? Read on!

If this book offers you more options, adds value to your life and supports you in your quest for the 'gold' at the end of your personal rainbow, you might join us in thanking:

- the team at learndirect, especially Kirstie Donnelly and Marion Reader, who shared the vision of a website to address career and life planning for the over 50s and made that vision a reality with **www.fiftyforward.co.uk**

- the web designers from The Workshop who worked their wizardry with the material we provided for that website and expanded it

- the team from Middlesex University Press, in particular Celia Cozens and Paul Jervis, who said let's make the material available to those who are happier with books rather than keyboards

- Jon Finegold for his patient editing

- Joseph Buckley for re-creating the Swamp diagram

- the many friends and family members whose lives are the models we learned from

- and the vast numbers of experts who share their material so generously via the miracle of the worldwide web and whose wisdom we drew upon.

The concept of gratitude figures prominently in this book so it is fitting that we should start with it.

We are vastly appreciative of all those who have encouraged, informed, inspired and challenged us, and the many more who have contributed to what follows in so very many ways without knowing they were doing so!

They have all helped us to design and find meaning in our own rainbow years, and for that we are very grateful!

Barrie Hopson and *Mike Scally*

Dr Barrie Hopson is a psychologist specialising in career development and lifelong learning. Beginning his paid work as a psychometrician working with the National Foundation for Educational Research, he soon moved to Leeds University as a researcher into vocational guidance. This was the beginning of a distinguished academic and commercial career. He established the Counselling and Career Development Unit at Leeds University in 1976 and subsequently went on to found Lifeskills International. He has authored over 25 books and set up five successful companies in the UK and one in the USA. He is currently chairman of Axia Interactive Media, and a non-executive director of two other companies. His books including the best-selling *12 Steps to Success through Service*, and *Build Your Own Rainbow*. The latter were all co-authored with Mike Scally. He was, with Mike, the subject matter expert for the learndirect website which reflects this current book.

Barrie has worked widely as a consultant to commercial and educational organisations in the UK, USA, Asia, Canada and Europe. He now enjoys a portfolio career as a writer, presenter, consultant and chair of his local community association. He has a wife, two grown up children, two small but disarming grandchildren and sees one of the major payoffs of his portfolio career as being able to follow Yorkshire County Cricket Club.

Mike Scally started his career in education, spending some twenty years in school and university teaching. After eight years as deputy director of the Counselling and Career Development Unit at Leeds University, he left to set up a people development company with Barrie Hopson. Mike was co-founder and eventually joint chairman of Lifeskills International, a company specialising in management development for major companies. He worked as both trainer and consultant, at all levels from board to front line in many major organisations.
In the mid 1990s Mike realised ICT would play an ever more significant role in individual and organisational development and negotiated a joint venture partnership company, CitizenConnect, with Axia Multimedia Corporation of Canada, becoming a consultant to both companies and eventually chairman of CitizenConnect. This company specialised in developing online learning programmes for major government and public bodies around the world.

Mike has written over twenty books (mostly co-authored with Barrie Hopson), and has lectured at many international management conferences on the themes of culture change, building customer-driven organisations, service excellence, career development, lifeskills teaching, learning organisations and self-managed learning. Mike has also consulted with organisations internationally, in Europe, Australia, Canada, Hong Kong, Scandinavia, Uganda and Brazil, and has a particular interest outside of business in making his expertise available to agencies working for development in the poorest areas of the Third World.

Mike has a grown up family of six and seven grandchildren and is enjoying a creative retirement.

To Valerie and Margaret
our partners in designing the future

Contents

Theme 7: My spirituality   **155**

Life transitions   **167**

Bringing it all together: where do you go from here?   **181**

Appendices   **193**

Introduction

'The rainbow years' – the pluses of being 50+

For the last 20 years, our book *Build Your Own Rainbow* has been a UK best-seller for those seeking to shape, or re-shape, their careers and their lives. We believe that many who used the book, and indeed many who didn't, could benefit now from a resource which equips them to design lives and careers at 50+ and meet the challenges of doing that in the very new circumstances that constitute the first part of the twenty-first century.

The first 'rainbow' book and the learning programmes and workshops based on it have been widely used across a range of organisations in the UK and elsewhere. Hundreds of people were trained to run workshops in organisations like ICI, BA, BBC, Rolls-Royce and Philips. Many more have had access to the process through computer software like CareerBuilder and learndirect Futures.

This new book is designed to help people in the generations over 50 to take greater charge of their lives and their careers, enabling them to make these more like they want them to be.

Who is this book for?

It is primarily for people of 50+ who are:

- Employed but considering a career change
- Employed but seeking a different work–life balance
- Self-employed or those considering self employment
- Unemployed but seeking a return to paid work
- Retired by choice, or by persuasion, and all points in-between
- Considering 'portfolio' living, with a balance of paid and unpaid work, leisure and community activities, learning and development.

What does the book offer?

We have designed and written it to provide the following:

- A 'toolbox' of thought-provoking and awareness-building activities and information to enhance life and career planning skills.
- Data gathered from people we have worked with and from questionnaires that people have completed prior to this project that may help to expand life and career choices. Reading what other people have planned and achieved might just suggest options not previously considered.
- A resource guide to expand life and career choices now and at points of career and life change in the future.
- Strategies for taking more control of one's life.
- A process for objective-setting and action-planning to shape the next stages of one's life and career.
- A resource for professionals who work with older adults on career and related issues. (Over the years we have received feedback from career guidance professionals telling us how useful they have found Build Your Own Rainbow in working with clients).
- A link to a learndirect website, www.fiftyforward.co.uk, based on this book and to which we contributed as subject matter experts.

Why 'rainbows' again?

We originally chose the rainbow as the symbol for our previous book because for many people it represents hope, beauty, optimism and enriching destinations. Fortunately, we believe that we do not have to wait for the rainbow elements to meet by chance. We believe that each of us can build our own rainbows. Part of rainbow mythology is the famed pot of gold supposedly to be found where the rainbow touches the earth. People who try to find those elusive pots of gold by chasing rainbows are often called day-dreamers with their heads in the clouds and hoping for impossible things.

There is little to gain from hoping for impossible things, but combining imagination with planning and research and using the results to shape our decision-making is the best way we know of converting impossible dreams into the realm of the possible.

True 'rainbow builders' know that the treasure lies within ourselves, waiting to be extracted and shaped into possibilities constrained only by the limits of our own imaginations.

Be a rainbow builder not a rainbow chaser!

The additional reason that we have stayed with the rainbow is that it has seven colours and in this book we offer seven life themes to be addressed if we are to continue to build rainbows for ourselves and to help others build theirs. Each aspect of our lives interacts with, impacts on and affects all other aspects. Our work is not detached from our learning, nor from our relationships, nor our leisure; none of these is unaffected by our financial position, and so on. It is difficult to isolate any aspect of us without producing ripples into our whole circumstance. In shaping our lives we need to fit the pieces together to get the whole picture.

Challenges of the twenty-first century for rainbow building

The twenty-first century brings new challenges for many reasons:

- The old model of a 'job for life' and then retirement is largely extinct. Changes in longevity are challenging the way we view paid work. For much of the twentieth century people worked long hours for most of their lives. Retirement was often short lived. Over the last decade or so many people have been retiring earlier and living longer, thereby considerably extending their 'retirement' time. This century is likely to curtail that, as many people will need to be in paid (though not necessarily full-time) work for much longer. They may still have relatively short 'retirements' in the old sense of freedom from full-time paid work.

- The over 50s not only live longer, are healthier and wealthier, they are also more numerous and have more life and career options than any previous generation. On reaching 50 today, people could have up to 50 years to work, live, plan for and enjoy. They are the 'regeneration generation', with opportunities for reinventing themselves in ways never possible before in our history.

- Pensions, and the certainty of them, are not what they used to be. More people will have to work longer and the government of the day will have difficulty in selling this if it simply means that people will have to do more of the same. People may be more motivated to continue with paid work if it is within the context of a portfolio life, of which it is one part, and maybe not even the most important part, of that life. To live a portfolio life we need to think beyond simply having or not having a job. We need to combine a range of aspects of our lives, make flexibility our credo and develop a portfolio of skills and activities, some for sale and some to be used for other purposes.

- Age discrimination legislation means older people have equal opportunities to go on using the skills and experience that they have developed – and opportunities to develop new ones.

- Previous models of family, defined gender roles, life-long relationships and careers for life are giving way to new models of family and relationships and 'portfolio' lives and careers.

- 'Work–life' balance and quality of life are taking precedence for many over job status and financial reward.

- 'Security' no longer comes from an organisation, but from being marketable, transferable and always having alternatives. As management guru, Peter Drucker, puts it, 'Corporations once built to last like pyramids are now more like tents…. You can't design your life around a temporary structure.'

- The needs for income, structure, recognition, status, purpose, contacts, etc. which once were all met by having 'a job', can now be met from a range of sources.

- 'Permanence', in many areas of life, has been replaced by continual change, bringing a need for self-management, re-invention and knowing how to manage life transitions. People wedded to the notion of 'job monogamy' will be increasingly disappointed.

- The previous concept of 'life-stages' (a time for doing what is expected of one) has given way to the notion of writing one's own life script. We do not have to be restricted by the life-patterns of our parents and grandparents.

- New technology has transformed the world of work and ways of working and at the same time supports a proliferation of leisure options and lifestyle choices.

- Increasingly we have to harmonise a whole range of life-roles: child, parent, worker, partner, friend, carer, for example, making these successful, integrated and compatible.

- Living longer, for many, means being sandwiched between one's ageing parents and one's offspring – who are likely to stay dependent longer, and possibly will never be as well off as their parents.

- In addition to this, however well we plan, we have to be able to respond to and adjust to 'events' – positive and negative happenings which are unpredictable and which can radically change our lives. Most people at some point in their lives will experience something life-changing and unexpected. We cannot control that, but we can influence how we deal with the event and its consequences.

- Happiness or life-satisfaction is an outcome of successfully balancing many features of our unique lives and designing our future amidst a multitude of possibilities, in a life so complex as to be unrecognisable by our own parents and grandparents.

So what are the implications of this for the over 50s?

- Of all the people in the history of the world who ever reached 65 years of age, one half of them are alive today.

- Around 42% of the UK population is over fifty years old and this figure is expected to increase by a further 10% by 2041. In economic terms, allowing employees to continue to develop their careers into later life will clearly be necessary, as well as hugely beneficial to both individual employers and the nation and economy as a whole.

- Our population is ageing: people aged 85 and over represented only 1.6% of the 50+ population in 1951, but represented 5.5% in 2003 – and are projected to be 9.1% in 2031.

- Women outnumber men at older ages, but the imbalance is projected to decrease in the future.

If you are just 50+, you may have lived only half of your life by now. This book will help you to look at the second half and design various aspects of your future.

'The best way to predict the future is to create it.'

Peter Drucker

There are now 20 million of us, the over 50s, and we are wealthier, healthier and busier than any comparable generation in human history.

Consequently, we over 50s, unlike any previous generation, probably have greater opportunity to take charge of our lives and make them more like we want them to be.

We have more **freedom**:

- from **geographic constraints** – we now have much more choice about where we want to live and even which country we wish to live in

- from **chronic health conditions** – we are healthier than any previous generation

- from **age stereotyping** – although there is a long way to go here, older people cannot be categorised today in the way that was easy in past generations.

'Guessing someone's age becomes increasingly difficult either through greater attention to personal appearance, fashion or even plastic surgery and less invasive cosmetic techniques. People in their 50s are sometimes parents of young children, sometimes grandparents, sometimes both. The average age of a Harley Davidson owner is 46!'

Heather Nicholson, The Times, 2004

Today *age* is definitely not an indication of lifestyle. *Attitude is*.

With the freedoms listed above come **challenges**:

- Many have to cope with being part of the 'sandwich generation'; having responsibilities at the same time for both children and elderly parents.

- Having to juggle and balance our range of life roles.

There are some specific areas we should consider:

- **Economic:** as we will be living much longer we will need more money for longer; fortunately, as a group those over 50 own 80% of the country's wealth.

- **Relationships:** 'til death us do part' can now mean an additional decade or so; divorce rates have risen significantly faster in the over 50s than in any other age group in the last 20 years.

- **Intellectual:** we will need to go on learning; if we don't, we will rust out or be left behind.

- **New technology:** we all now need to be able to deal with computers, mobile phones, DVDs, digital TV, increasingly complicated household equipment and microchips with everything.

- **Psychological:** how do we avoid a sense of unimportance if, eventually, we lose an occupational identity?

But there are also **opportunities** to:

- Design the next 30+ years of our lives
- Develop new careers
- Find a balance between paid and unpaid work and the range of life roles that we play
- Find new activities and interests
- Learn new things
- Travel more
- Make a contribution to the community
- Create new models for living
- Develop a new identity
- Exercise greater political power.

> *'Don't let age get in the way of ambition.'*
>
> *Klaus, in his 50s*

It's also time to dream

We may not associate dreaming dreams with later years, but an interesting piece of research carried out by Unmissable Ltd, a company which has set out to offer its clients a chance to make their dreams come true, suggests otherwise. A questionnaire and focus groups found the peak 'dreaming ages' proved to be the very young and the seriously mature. Adolescence, unsurprisingly, is the great age for making lists of what you are going to do with your life, with 70% of teenagers writing down life goals. But at 55 the wish list comes out again, with 64% of this age group keeping a list of plans, which is revised, updated and used as an agenda for the rest of life.

This book is our contribution to helping you to revisit your dreams and make the rest of your life more like you want it to be.

> *'We cannot live the afternoon of life according to the programmes of life's morning.'*
>
> *CJ Jung*

> *'Clarify what for you will mean that, when you die, you will feel you have had a successful life – then do something towards this each day.'*
>
> *Mike Pegg, in his 60s*

You really *can* create your own future, revisit your rainbows, identify new ones and move on from your past. This book can help you to do that and more.

> *Remember, just because you have grown up does not mean that you have stopped growing!*

Before we introduce you to the seven life themes we will invite you to assess:

'My story so far...'

This will be an opportunity to assess your life and your career so far and to project ahead. You will explore what *age* and *ageing* means to you. You will examine your achievements and experiences to date and draw out the learning from these, which can help you shape your preferred future. You will examine the returns that you get from how you currently invest your time and energy. A range of diagnostics and activities will help build a picture of your transferable skills, interests and life values. The vital distinction is made here between paid and unpaid work. The invitation is to explore just what you might like 'more of',' less of' or indeed wish to keep the 'same', in career and life terms at this stage. This picture will be expanded as you continue to build or rebuild your unique rainbow.

> *'Only look back to learn, never with regret; concentrate on what you can achieve in the future.'*
>
> *Ian Walker, in his 50s*

The seven life themes

The seven life themes that will influence and impact on our decisions are:

- My work options
- My finances
- My relationships
- My learning
- My health and wellbeing
- My leisure
- My spirituality

'My work options'

This theme is split into four sections and explores the options in paid work, unpaid work, patterns of employment and retirement. The advantages and disadvantages of each option will be explored; a link will be made between your self-assessed skills, interests and values and a wide range of job families. We examine the growing alternatives to full-time paid work and ask you to reflect on the different options for flexible working that are now mushrooming. Traditionally a job provided, to different degrees, income, structure, purpose, status, esteem, human contact, respect in the community, an opportunity to use our skills and learning. We need to ask if these needs can be met in other ways. We all need work – but it can be paid or unpaid.

For those seeking paid work, the latest data from the Office of National Statistics are comforting: over 40% of the jobs created in 2006 were filled by people over pensionable age.

'My finances'

Any vision we develop for our life is likely to be affected by the resources available to us. This theme will ask you to reflect on, and work out answers to, questions such as:

- What are your current resources?

- What are your financial liabilities?

- Given your needs, values, responsibilities, dependents and likely longevity, how much do you need to live on, now and in the future?

- Do you spend or save? And if 'save', then for what?

- Could you afford a 'portfolio' life?

- Do you need to earn more to achieve your ambitions– if so how?

- How will you live in retirement, if it ever happens? Are you investing in ways that are compatible with your vision?

- What do you not know that you need to know?

- Who else do you need to share this analysis with?

'My relationships'

This theme explores the place of relationships in our lives and their links with life-satisfaction and health. There is data which clearly links positive relationships to wellbeing. Most people have significant relationships in their lives that hopefully add a very positive dimension to everything they plan or undertake. For some however, the significant relationship brings challenge, a need for re-evaluation and adjustments in ambitions. This theme will help you to explore:

- The key relationships in your life.

- The contribution they make to happiness in life.

- Your support system: who can you go to for support, encouragement, challenge, feedback?

- Do you need to expand or change this in any way?

'My learning'

Lifelong learning is a concept that today goes unchallenged. The previous model of 'front-loading' education (we went to school/college/university and then were thought to be 'educated for life'), was superseded in the last quarter of the twentieth century. Now, the realisation is that the world is changing so fast that 'up-skilling' and re-engagement with learning is indeed a life-long requirement. What also went was the notion that learning was simply to prepare us for work. Today we have to commit to learning and renewing ourselves to enable us to stay relevant and 'marketable', but also to enable us to enjoy our development for its own sake. Many over 50s are taking up FE and HE courses, because now they are at a stage of their lives when they have the time and the resources to experience the adventure of learning for its own sake.

This theme will help you identify your preferred style of learning and your favoured methods of learning to better equip you for the life ahead.

'My health and wellbeing'

This theme reminds us of the implications of health and fitness for life choices. There is material for assessing aspects of fitness and wellbeing, to be considered alongside career and life aspirations. There will be information on research linking diet, exercise and lifestyle to wellbeing and longevity. Again, signposts and examples will be provided for many areas of health and fitness improvement.

'My leisure'

There are unprecedented leisure options for the 50+ age group many of whom are 'time and money rich', having spent their last three decades committed to career-building and/or family-raising. Having reached

50+, many may need to re-learn how to 'play' or even 'adventure'. This section will invite exploration of, and answers to, questions such as:

- How much 'non-work' time do you have?
- What do you do with it ('chill'; hobbies; exercise; sport; learning or what)?
- What are you getting out of your leisure time?
- Is it what you are looking for, is it enough?
- Who else might be affected by your decisions?
- What might you be missing?
- What's new out there that you might try?
- What do you want to do about it?

'My spirituality'

For our age group it can be of great interest to re-examine the bigger questions of life:

- What's it all about?
- Why are we here?
- Does life have any greater meaning or purpose?
- How should we be living now – to be part of the solution and not part of the problem?

While there may have been a decline in traditional church attendances, there has been an expansion of interest in other areas with a spiritual dimension, such as new age living; meditation; peace movements; holistic medicine; environmental concerns; work for charities; one-world development; ethical living without religion.

This theme will ask you to examine whether spirituality has meaning for you and, if so, how it might be integrated into life and career planning.

In addition to these seven life themes, there is also a section that we call:

'Life transitions'

> *John Lennon said that, 'life is what happens to you when you are busy making plans.'*

There are many things and events in life that we can predict and plan for, but there are others that take us by surprise and can dramatically impact our quality of life[1]: an adult child dies, a partner wants a divorce

after many years together; grandchildren suddenly require looking after because a parent cannot cope, goes to prison, chooses to work abroad; we have to face redundancy; we lose a pension, etc.

On the positive side, there may be an invitation to return to quality work again, long after this was expected; we may have unanticipated opportunities to travel; grandchildren arrive after we assumed this was never going to happen; we rediscover old friends who bring a new dimension to living, etc. This theme explores the generic nature of life transitions, enables you to assess your transition coping style and suggests ways of managing any transition more effectively.

Finally, you are asked to bring together all of your reflections and work which will enable you to plan how you can get a balance between your life themes. This concluding section is called 'Bringing it all together'. You will be asked to set objectives and make action plans to shape the next phase of your life and your career. You will be able to build new rainbows for yourself and others.

Throughout the book we will be alert to how technology is expanding our options and our choices in so many fields. It can contribute to an overwhelming feeling of information and choice overload, but can also help us explore options, get information when we need it and help us to make decisions that shape our life.

Personal stories

In preparation for the learndirect website and for this book, we emailed out around 150 questionnaires (reproduced in Appendix 4). Throughout the book you will find quotations from responses we received. Some people have given their real names whereas others have preferred to use a pseudonym. In addition, we have quotations and reflections collected over a 20-year period, from the thousands of people who have taken part in workshops designed around the original Build Your Own Rainbow process; where appropriate for the over 50s, we have also drawn on these rich veins of data.

Many of the people who have filled in these questionnaires have commented on how useful this was in getting them to think about all of the issues raised under the seven life themes.

---

1 These are all examples gleaned from the responses to our questionnaire.

To get the most out of this book:

- We strongly recommend that you begin with *'My story so far…'*. We have designed a very flexible process which we hope makes it clear that how you tackle this project is up to you. If leisure is your big challenge right now, then start with that. If retirement is your preoccupation, then you might not want to spend time on the 'work options' theme. You're over 50 – you will do what you want anyway! We are just trying to make the process more flexible for you.

- Be honest with yourself. This will help to get you to where you want to be and save you much time.

- Recognise that the process will not give you 'answers' in the sense of definite directives about what is best for you. No learning programme can know or do enough to define what is best for someone as unique as you. There has never been anyone with your unique combination of genes, upbringing, education, experiences, thoughts, values, contacts, relationships. So what you will find here are *clues* and *options* for you to consider, rather than prescriptions or instructions.

- You will, however, find 'answers' in the thoughts that the material stimulates in you. Many people find that, when they embark on this process, they experience moments of real insight or, if you like, an 'Aha! moment'. Be alert to things about yourself that occur to you as you work. At the back of the book are some blank pages which we call 'Aha!' pages. Harvest your insights and record them here: they could be important clues to things you want to work on, change or achieve. Any 'dawnings', realisations about what you like or dislike, what you want or don't want, what changes you might want or not want, are important data for you to capture. Be very alert to the things you become aware of, about yourself, about your preferences, your aspirations and ambitions as you work through the activities or reflect on them later. When it comes to the final chapter of 'Bringing it all together' we will ask you to re-visit the contents of your 'Aha!' pages and use them as an aid to objective setting. For some people, the pages will not provide sufficient space – so for them a good notebook will be essential.

- This is a book to be 'used' and not just read. Write in it. Make notes. Capture your realisations!

Each theme consists of:

- An **introduction** to the topic.
- **'Do you know?':** a potpourri of facts, research and viewpoints, which could illuminate this topic for you as you work through it.

- **Activities:** pauses for directed thought, which will help you to collect data about yourself; these pieces of data will be the building blocks for your future. Activities are numbered within each theme (e.g. Activity 3.2, which would be the second activity in Theme 3). Activities in the three other sections are numbered separately

- **How to find out more** about that theme. As well as referring you to the learndirect website (**www.fiftyforward.co.uk**) for the most up-to-date information, we will give you some generic reference points. In addition we will recommend a selection of words and phrases that we have found useful, with search engines such as Google.

- A **review** of what you have done and what you have learned.

- Setting some **objectives and action plans** for yourself.

Throughout all the sections you will see **quotations from people** whom we have surveyed, interviewed or talked to on career and life planning workshops.

Working with someone else

We strongly hope that many of you will use this opportunity to connect with others working their way through the same programme. Talking through your thinking with others can help you to refine and clarify your ideas and motivate you. Also, their reactions, responses, and challenges are likely to be valuable and stimulating – and provide you with even more food for thought.

Additionally, talking over your ideas with somebody you trust can really help you to clarify your thoughts, even if they themselves are not working through the process at the time.

We like to use the phrase, 'It takes 2 to see 1'. It can sometimes be enlightening to involve family, friends and colleagues in contributing their perspectives as you work on some of the activities. It could also be scary!

You could do this online at the learndirect website (**www.fiftyforward.co.uk**) or simply find someone you know who would like to work through this programme with you. With emails, telephone and social media sites, this is now easier than it ever was.

Who knows – you may even choose to meet up face to face, once in a while!

You could consider forming a small group to do this. There are 'book clubs' after all, so why not a 'life and career planning' club?

When you do link up with fellow rainbow builders, you should establish a clear 'contract' between yourselves. Discuss and agree:

- How you will communicate together

- How often you will communicate

- How you will make contact

- What work you will talk through or compare notes on

- Whether you are prepared to open this up to other rainbow builders

- What kind of help you will find most useful and what kind of help you will not want; rules about confidentiality; about how you share time; about agreed times of contact etc.

Barrie and Mike have also started a blog to follow up on any developments relevant to *The Rainbow Years* that excite or impress them. For ongoing information, statistics, research or just current stories that get us thinking or laughing, log on and subscribe to **www.theplusesofbeing50plus.blogspot.com**

When we wrote *Build Your Own Rainbow* the internet had not been developed, so almost one-fifth of the book consisted of resources. Today, as soon as we recommend a source of help, a website, an organisation, etc., the information will most likely be out of date by the time this book is printed. The web has changed all of this, which is why this book has general directions and suggestions, but a minimum of time-limited resource material.

We want the 'fiftyforward' website to be the first choice website for people over 50 designing their own futures. It will be updated from time to time with new information, interesting and useful links, case studies and research. It will offer a networking opportunity in which users can communicate with one another online or even arrange face-to-face meetings if desired.

You will be able to link up with other people who have done or are doing the same programme and who are keen to communicate with others who are going through similar experiences. For example, if you have to deal with moving a parent into residential housing you might find it useful to communicate online with others who are doing the same. You may be trying to start up your own business and are looking for someone to partner with. You may be thinking of a particular career change and would love to talk with someone who has done it, or considering volunteering and would like to hear from people who have chosen to do different things, etc.

We are still building rainbows for ourselves and hopefully still helping others to build them for themselves. We are still creating our own futures and have produced this book to support you in creating yours. We wish each of you a very creative future!

Barrie Hopson and *Mike Scally*

My story so far...

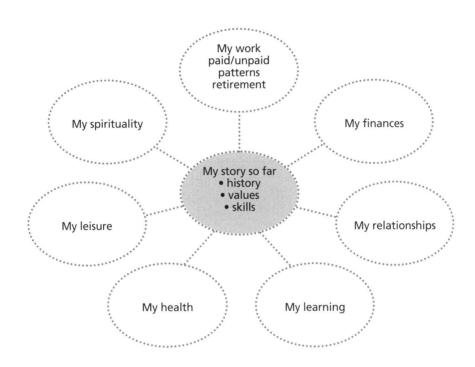

Introduction

This theme will offer you an opportunity to review your life and your career so far and then invite you to begin to project ahead. We are encouraging you to embark on a journey to create your own future for the second part of your life.

You will:

- Explore the concept of age and ageing as it affects you

- Examine your achievements and experiences to date, drawing out the learning from these to help you create your future

- Reflect on the unplanned events that have happened to you and examine what you did to benefit from them or what more you might have done

- Keep a record of how you currently invest your time and identify the returns you are getting from this

- Assess your life values, your transferable skills and your interests that remain the foundation for the next phase of your life and career

- Be asked to explore just what you might like 'more of', 'less of' or indeed wish to keep the 'same', in life and career terms at this stage. This picture will be expanded as you continue to build your unique future through the rest of this programme.

At any point in our life we are on a bridge between:

- **Our history** – which we can't change

- **Our future** – which we can shape!

We are balanced between achievement and potential, between experience, learning, accomplishments and untapped capacity still to be developed. A teacher we knew used to challenge students who said 'I can't do…' to replace that statement with 'I haven't learned to do… yet!' The first statement stops us from developing ourselves. The second clearly states that we are capable of so much more. We are never 'over'. We should never put a full-stop after ourselves and recognising that prepares us to look at our future creatively.

> *'Some men see things as they are and say, "Why?" I dream of things that never were and say, "Why not?"'*
>
> *George Bernard Shaw*

Do you know?

Professor Tom Kirkwood, director of CISBAN, said: 'Life expectancy is still growing by a staggering five hours a day. This has been happening for the past 20–30 years and we do not know when this will stop or slow down. The old idea that we had a predetermined life span as a species has been shown to be plain wrong'.

- By 2025, more than a third of the UK's population will be over 55. We are living longer, healthier and more active lives.

- Crystallised intelligence – which relates to the storage of information such as vocabulary and general knowledge – increases with age.

- Fluid intelligence – which relates to the rapid processing of information in problem solving – does decline steadily, but by how much will depend upon whether we continue to stretch and exercise our brain.

- It is a myth that advancing age alone will cause memory loss. There is a real difference in chronological and biological age. Many people reach a very advanced age with little, if any, problem with memory loss.

- Older people are living younger – ever more involved in sports and exercise, ever more sociable, ever more adventurous and in search of new experiences. In many ways their lifestyles have come to resemble those of younger people 50 years ago.

Martin Lloyd-Elliott[2], psychologist, comments: 'While our modern society is apparently so biased towards youth culture, a more radical and transformative change has occurred amongst the over fifties that leaves teenagers lagging behind. Today, 50 is closer to the middle of our life than to its end, with many economic and psychological factors bringing this change. Psychologically, there has been a shift from a 'closing down' expectation for the second half of life towards a much more optimistic 'opening up of new doors' spirit of good times ahead.'

> *'90% of the world's woe comes from people not knowing themselves, their abilities, their frailties, and even their real virtues. Most of us go almost all the way through life as complete strangers to ourselves.'*
>
> *Sidney Harris*

> *Beryl Markham, the famous aviator, said that people can live a lifetime and know other people better than they know themselves.*

2 Quote from 'Why 50 somethings live like 20 somethings.', Rosemary Bennett, *The Times*, May 2007.

Activity 1

Who was I, who am I and who will I be?

This activity demonstrates that life is a process of change and development.

■ **Think of yourself ten years ago.** Imagine you had to give someone a description of who you were at that time. Write down what you would say about yourself as you were then. Think about the job you were doing, the friends and or partner you had, your family circumstances, your health and appearance, your hobbies or leisure activities, where you lived, the kind of holidays you took, any learning you were engaged in, your financial position and so on. Write it in the first person and in the present tense – as if it was still you – 'I am… I believe… I like….etc.'

_____
_____
_____
_____
_____
_____
_____
_____
_____
_____
_____
_____
_____
_____
_____
_____
_____
_____
_____
_____
_____
_____

■ **Think of yourself now.** How would you complete that same task now? Write in your pen portrait of yourself as you are now.

_____
_____
_____
_____
_____
_____

_____
_____
_____
_____
_____
_____
_____
_____
_____
_____
_____
_____
_____
_____
_____
_____
_____

■ **Now think ten years into the future.** What might you be like then? In physical appearance, in job and career, in relationships, in financial status, in your leisure activities and so on. Write in your new description – again in the first person, as if you were living at this time.

_____
_____
_____
_____
_____
_____
_____
_____
_____
_____
_____
_____
_____
_____
_____
_____
_____
_____
_____
_____
_____
_____

■ Reflecting on yourself at those three different stages, what do you realise? What differences are there over that 20-year period, in you and in your world?

_____

_____

_____

_____

_____

_____

_____

_____

_____

_____

_____

_____

_____

_____

_____

_____

_____

_____

_____

_____

_____

When people have completed this activity on our workshops, they typically note that:

• Change happens – it is part of life and unavoidable

• Some of that change may have been desirable – e.g. greater financial security – and some will have not been what you wanted – e.g. loss of job or relationship

• Some of the changes you will have chosen and some will have happened without you choosing them. We can shape some things in our lives and some we don't have too much choice about.

■ Some people feel more comfortable reflecting back on what has been. Others prefer to focus on the future. Some are only comfortable with what is now. Which of these statements sums you up?

_____

_____

_____

_____

_____

_____

[end activity]

The last activity asked you to learn from the past. One of our beliefs is that:

'There is no future in the past.'

We can reflect upon it, we can learn from it, but we can't change it. So, it is important we don't dwell in the past. What is gone is gone, not to be dismissed or denied but to be seen as a launch pad for what comes next. What we always have is an opportunity to make our future more like we want it to be.

> *'Personal growth can be viewed as making new connections in any of several directions: UPWARD to achieve one's full potential; OUTWARD to make contact and encounter others; INWARD to increase our awareness of who we are, and what we want, need, sense, feel, think, and do; and DOWNWARD to touch earth, to be grounded, and to connect.'*
>
> *Giges and Rosenfeld* [3]

> *'Every second we live is a unique moment of the universe, a moment that never was before and never will be again. And what do we teach our children in school? We teach them that 2 and 2 make 4 and Paris is the capital of France. We should say to each of them, 'Do you know who you are? You are a marvel! In the millions of years that have passed there has never been any one like you!'*
>
> *Pablo Casals*

3 Quoted in *Reviewing Skills Training,* Roger Greenaway, 2004.
www.reviewing.co.uk/outdoor

Activity 2

How old am I?

> *'I don't feel 75, nearer 60, though with less energy.'*
>
> *Mary, in her 70s*

According to marketing agency Millennium, many people aged between 50 and 60 actually feel 10–15 years younger than their age. Is this true for you?

Fill in the gaps in the following sentences:

1. I judge my body to be like that of a person about _____ years of age.

2. My thoughts and interests are like those of a person about _____.

3. My position in society is like that of a person about _____.

4. Deep down inside, I really feel like a person about _____.

5. In other people's eyes, I look as though I am about _____.

6. I honestly would prefer to be about _____ years of age.

Reflect on that activity and write in your thoughts on the following:

■ What do my answers say about me and how I see myself?

_____

_____

_____

_____

_____

■ What does it say about how I regard ageing?

_____

_____

_____

_____

_____

■ What might be the consequences for me of my attitudes to ageing?

_____

_____

_____

_____

_____

_____

[end activity]

Probably, if you are like most people, you will not have given the same age for all of the questions. That is because age is so very much more than a biological process. It is a highly charged topic with emotional and social significance. Age discrimination has become such a prominent issue because so many of us are living longer and want to work (whether paid or not), learn, do new things and, yes, even take risks.

'Only after we understand the profound significance of the epochs in our lives can we understand the ways in which one is, at a single time, a child, a youth, a middle-aged and an elderly person. We are never ageless. As we gain a greater sense of our own biographies, however, we can begin to exist at multiple ages. In the process we do not fragment ourselves, rather we become more integrated and whole.'

Daniel Levinson [4]

If you click on **www.realage.com** by answering their questions you can work out the difference between your actual chronological age and your biological age based on your health and lifestyle. The site also gives you suggestions as to how you can bring your biological age down. The website is American so some of the medical questions may need some translation. We like this site as we both came out as considerably younger than we really are!

4 Levinson,D.J.,Darrow,C.N.,Klein,B.,Levinson,M.H.,& Mckee,B. _The Seasons of a Man's Life_, New York, Alfred Knopf, 1978

Activity 3

My lifeline

Part 1

Use a large sheet of paper. Across the middle draw a line to represent around 100 years. 0 is the point of your birth at one end and 100 years at the other (unless you are already a centenarian and need a longer line – in which case congratulations!). Put an X on the line to show where you are now. Your past is to the left of the X – your future to the right. At intervals write in next to the line the key events in your life so far. Use both sides of the line. Start with events as early as you can remember and proceed to the present.

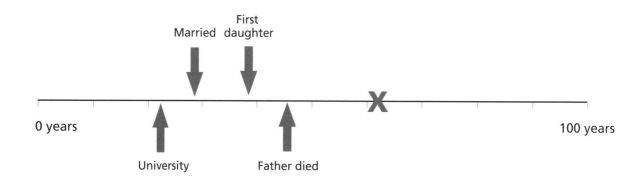

Leave plenty of space between the years. You will find that one memory triggers off another, so be prepared to move back and forth along the line as the memories flow back to you.

Part 2

When you have completed your lifeline – and remember you can always add new events as they occur to you – ask yourself the following questions for each event and put the appropriate symbol or symbols next to each event. For some, none of the following symbols might apply, so do improvise if necessary.

1. Was this a **peak experience** (a highly positive experience?) Mark with a **P**
2. Was this a **trough experience** (a personal low time?) Mark with a **T**
3. Was this event **unexpected**? Mark with a **U**
4. How **stressful** was this event for me? Mark with **S** (somewhat) or **SS** (stressful) or **SSS** (very stressful)
5. Did I take any **risks**? If so at which points? Mark with an **R**
6. Was there important **learning** in this for me? Mark with an **L**
7. Which key events were **planned**?   Mark with a *****
8. Which key events were **unplanned**?   Mark with a **!**
9. Looking at your lifeline, what would you say have been your three major achievements or things you are most proud to have done? Circle those or highlight them.

Take as much time as you need to do this – after all this is your life!

Part 3

Now, reflect further on your lifeline and answer the following questions:

■ What does this account of your life say about you and how you have lived your life so far?

_____

_____

_____

■ Does anything surprise you?

_____

_____

_____

■ What are the most important elements or features in your peak experiences?

_____

_____

_____

■ What are the most important elements or features in your trough experiences?

_____

_____

_____

■ What have you learned from your peak experiences?

_____

_____

_____

■ What have you learned from your trough experiences?

_____

_____

_____

■ What is your approach to risk-taking? Has risk-taking turned out mostly positive or negative for you?

_____

_____

_____

■ Are there any changes in the pattern of your life with age?

_____

_____

_____

■ What are the unfinished themes in your life?

_____

_____

_____

■ Now focus on those significant events which were unplanned. How have unplanned events influenced your life and your career?

_____

_____

_____

■ Overall, how well did you manage these events?

_____

_____

_____

■ Are there any examples of unplanned events which you were able to turn to your advantage and what did you gain?

_____

_____

_____

■ What have been your most important lessons from your life so far?

_____

_____

_____

Even at this early stage can you see:

■ anything you want to achieve in the time ahead?

_____

_____

_____

■ anything you want to be different?

_____

_____

_____

[end activity]

Luck has been defined as the crossroads where preparation and opportunity meet. There will always be unplanned events in life but the skill is in learning how to respond most effectively, in managing the changes that are necessary and then seeing how you might actually benefit from the new realities – even if initially some of them may not appear desirable.

Your use of time

What you have done so far is to step back and take a look at your life overall as you have lived it until now. The next step is to look in greater detail at just how you are investing your time.

It is not unusual for people to spend huge amounts of time analysing returns and payoffs from their investments, working out the 'best buy' for a freezer, DVD or brand of marmalade, or spending hours bidding on eBay – yet we quite often fail to transfer these considerable analytical skills to our own lives!

It can be very valuable to reflect regularly on:

- What returns am I getting for the time and energy I am investing?
- What parts of my life are my 'best buys'?
- How am I actually filling the hours of each day?
- What would it be good to change?

Activity 4

How do I spend my time?

Part 1

We know from research into weight control that most of us are notoriously unreliable when it comes to recalling what we eat and the same is true for how we spend our time. Consequently, we invite you to keep a record of your activities for what you think is a fairly typical week of your life.

It is best done by recording what you have done at the end of each day. You can fill in your time-log on the table provided here or create your own.

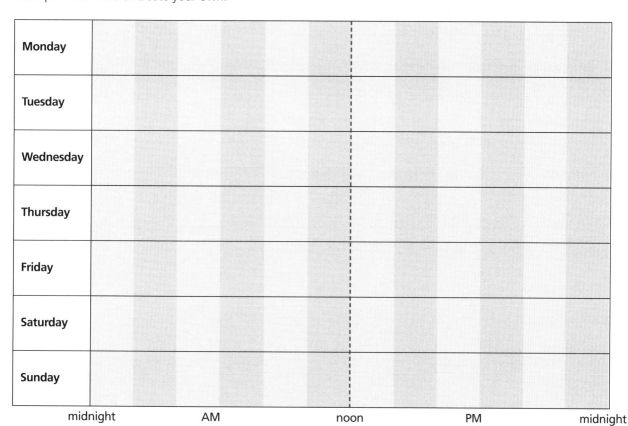

	midnight	AM	noon	PM	midnight
Monday					
Tuesday					
Wednesday					
Thursday					
Friday					
Saturday					
Sunday					

Part 2

After you have completed your time-log for a week, study it and then fill in your responses to the following questions:

■ How typical was this week?

_____

_____

_____

■ What does this snapshot tell me about the way I am spending my time?

_____

_____

_____

■ How much of my week was spent doing things I choose to do?

_____

_____

_____

■ What might I want to change?

_____

_____

_____

■ What are the most rewarding things I do that I would like to do more of?

_____

_____

_____

■ What are the least rewarding things that I would like to do less of?

_____

_____

_____

[end activity]

Your life values

Whenever we ask ourselves questions such as:

- how do I like to spend my time?
- what kind of people do I choose to have around me?
- where do I want to live and to work?
- how important to me is money, status, independence, creativity, making decisions, taking risks, helping others, security, success, etc.?

…we are asking ourselves questions about our values, those things that are important to us. Being able to answer questions like those above, therefore, will always be crucial to enable us to make our life more like we want it to be. The more we are able to live out our values the more rewarding our lives will be.

As we grow up we absorb 'messages' and influences from our parents, our families, our teachers, our friends and eventually from the media and the culture we engage with. We emerge as adults with our own selection of beliefs, preferences, priorities about what matters to us, what is most important for us to do, to be, to have, to aspire to, to work for. Each of us has a unique combination of values that influence and shape our decisions, our behaviours and perhaps even decide how satisfied and happy we will be with our lives and careers.

Values affect how we judge and evaluate our life and the experiences it presents us with. For example, if we value integrity we will not be happy in circumstances that involve deceit or double-dealing. If we prize challenge and adventure we are unlikely to survive in a routine or bureaucratic context. Living a life or following a career that is aligned with our values is much more likely to result in high levels of satisfaction, motivation, commitment, health and wellbeing and possibly happiness.

> *'I have come to realise that work is something that's important in itself rather than a necessary way to earn a living. Work brings its own fulfilment and in a way is crucial to being human.'*
>
> *Denise, in her 50s*

We may be highly competent in a particular area, but if what we are doing is not in line with our values it may well not be that satisfying.

Our values become apparent early on in life and are more stable than attitudes, interests and transferable skills. Our values are what drive us and motivate us to do and not to do certain things and to make choices every day.

Activity 5

What are my life values?

This activity will provide an opportunity for you to identify your key life values.

It will:

- Invite you to reflect on values that people have said are influential in life generally and decide how much they might apply to you
- Ask you to identify values that may not be included here but you know influence your decisions and your choices every day
- Ask you to identify up to eight life values that are most important to you and how your life currently measures up to them.

Part 1

Appendix 1 consists of 40 cards, which you can cut out. You may wish to photocopy the pages first, and cut out the copy.

There are 32 **life value** cards and also 5 **descriptor** cards with the following headings/note:

1. VERY IMPORTANT
   This is very important to me and drives many of my decisions and actions.

2. IMPORTANT
   This is important to me and definitely affects what I decide and what I do.

3. QUITE IMPORTANT
   This is quite important to me and shapes some of my decisions.

4. OF SOME IMPORTANCE
   This is of little importance to me.

5. NOT IMPORTANT
   This is not one of my values and has no influence on what I pursue or how I operate.

You will also find 3 **blank** cards. If you think that some of your values are missing from the printed set, then please write them in on these blanks.

Part 2

Place the five heading cards in front of you as indicated:

VERY IMPORTANT	IMPORTANT	QUITE IMPORTANT	OF SOME IMPORTANCE	NOT IMPORTANT

Look at the first of the 32 life value cards, and ask yourself the question:

■ *How important is this value in my life as a whole? How much does it shape my decisions and my actions?*

Place the value under the group heading which best describes how important that value is to you. Work through the rest of the cards in turn, placing each one in the group that best describes how important that value is in your life

Part 3

After sorting all of the cards into these five groups, it will be helpful to ensure you have between 4 and a maximum of 8 in the VERY IMPORTANT column. If there are more than 8, we would suggest that you examine the cards again, to refine your priority values further.

When you have the cards in five groups, look at each group in turn. Arrange the cards so that in each category you rank order the cards from the most to the least important.

Part 4

Appendix 2 consists of a table in which you can record your VERY IMPORTANT values and also your NOT IMPORTANT values. The latter are important, so that later you can assess how much doing things that you do not value might just be part of your job or your life.

[end activity]

With your list of key life values you now have a tool that you can use to analyse the suitability of any key life decision – about choosing or accepting a job, choosing unpaid work or a particular pattern of employment, or whether or not to retire. Theme 1, 'My work options', will give you an opportunity of doing just that.

Transferable skills

Traditionally, our society has been pre-occupied with the skills essential for, or related to, a particular job: job-specific skills. Examples of these would be:

- A car mechanic, with a set of skills and knowledge around fixing and repairing cars or engines

- A doctor, who has skills and knowledge of medicine and its use in healing people

- A chef, who has skills related to the preparation of food.

These are examples of skills which are learned for, and applied to, a particular task.

In today's working world, less emphasis is being placed on job-specific skills and more on the transferable skills we can apply to a range of occupations and our other life roles. The thinking behind this is that people can be easily trained to acquire job-related skills, but if an employee is unable to communicate effectively, manage their time or work with others, etc., he or she will not be a desirable or effective contributor – no matter how much job-specific training they receive.

All of this is equally true for unpaid work and voluntary activities.

Activity 6

My transferable skills

Appendix 3 contains 56 cards describing transferable skills. You will also find 4 header cards with the following descriptions:

- **Very competent**
- **Competent**
- **Adequate**
- **Undeveloped.**

Part 1

Cut out the cards (again, you may wish to copy the pages first).

Place the four header cards in front of you and sort out the rest under them by asking yourself:

■ *'Which of these skills can I perform very competently, competently, adequately or which have I not yet developed?'*

Place each card under the appropriate header.

Some of the skills which you have not yet developed you may, of course, never have a desire to do so, but some you may be interested in developing at some future time.

Part 2

Write down, in the 'My transferable skills' table, all of the skills at which you have assessed yourself as being VERY COMPETENT and COMPETENT.

My transferable skills table

Very competent	Competent	Want to use a great deal	Skills I would like to develop
		Want to use sometimes	
		Want to use rarely or never	

Look back at the skills in the COMPETENT, ADEQUATE and UNDEVELOPED columns. Are there any of these in which you would like to develop greater competence?

Write these down in the table where indicated.

Part 3

Take your VERY COMPETENT and COMPETENT skills and sort them into three piles indicating those which you:

WANT TO USE	WANT TO USE	WANT TO USE
A GREAT DEAL	SOMETIMES	RARELY OR NEVER

The skills you have identified as your VERY COMPETENT ones and WANT TO USE A GREAT DEAL are your **most transferable** skills.

The skills you have identified as your COMPETENT ones and which you WANT TO USE A GREAT DEAL are your next most transferable skills.

Not wanting to use these skills does not necessarily make them non-transferable, although we have found that people are less likely to look for opportunities which involve skills they are less motivated to use.

Part 4

Each of the cards has a word on it, either:

DATA   IDEAS   PEOPLE   THINGS

These are the four main groupings of transferable skills.

Ask yourself:

■ *"How many of my transferable skills are in each of the categories?"*

Count the cards in the different categories and write the totals in the squares below:

DATA   IDEAS   PEOPLE   THINGS

DATA
If you have a high score in DATA skills, typically you enjoy working with figures and systems. You also tend to enjoy routine and are able to evaluate and organise facts or data about goods and services. These are highly valued skills in the labour market and as a result there are a wide range of occupations available to you at all levels.

IDEAS
Being high in IDEA skills reflects the fact that you enjoy experimenting with words, figures and music as well as being involved in developing new models and systems. These skills are increasingly attractive to the labour market and to organisations who want to distinguish themselves from their competitors by offering innovative products or services. As a result there could be lots of occupations available to you at all levels.

PEOPLE
A high score in PEOPLE skills means that there is a wide range of occupations available to you that require people who like to help, serve and entertain people as well as those which involve informing, teaching, persuading, motivating, selling to and directing other people. People who have a high score in this area are likely to enjoy working for changes in other people's behaviour as well as helping others.

THINGS
A high score in THINGS shows you have the skills to operate in a working environment where you will make, repair and service things. You are also likely to be attracted to work that is related to transport, manufacturing, construction, engineering or working with computers. People who score high in this area tend to like using tools or machinery or new technologies and want to understand how things work.

[end activity]

In the theme on work you will have an opportunity to link your transferable skills to paid and unpaid work options.

Activity 7

My interests

Your interests represent your preferences for doing some activities rather than others. Some people like cooking, others like driving cars, some like blogging, others like to paint or read books or do voluntary work.

Psychologists have suggested that people's interests incline them to particular types of paid or unpaid work. This exercise is based on the work of John Holland who also found that people in the same occupation, although they may have different values, will have similar skills and interests (J.L. Holland, *Making Vocational Choices: A Theory of Careers*, Englewood Cliffs, Prentice Hall, 1973).

Here are six sets of statements. For each of them, show how much you agree or disagree with the statement by circling a number from 1 to 5 (1 being 'highly disagree' and 5 being 'highly agree'.)

Interests – group P

I like fixing and repairing things	1	2	3	4	5
I like to keep fit	1	2	3	4	5
I like making things with my hands	1	2	3	4	5
I like doing things outdoors	1	2	3	4	5
I like hard, physical work	1	2	3	4	5
I enjoy working with tools and machines	1	2	3	4	5
Add up the numbers				**Total for P =**	

Interests – group FO

I like to understand things thoroughly	1	2	3	4	5
I like exploring new ideas	1	2	3	4	5
I enjoy working on problems	1	2	3	4	5
I like asking questions	1	2	3	4	5
I like learning about new things	1	2	3	4	5
I like to work out my own answers to problems	1	2	3	4	5
Add up the numbers				**Total for FO =**	

Interests – group A

I like seeing art shows, plays and good films	1	2	3	4	5
I like to be different	1	2	3	4	5
I forget about everything else when I'm being creative	1	2	3	4	5
It is vital to have beautiful and unusual things around me	1	2	3	4	5
I like to use my imagination	1	2	3	4	5
I like expressing myself through writing, painting or music	1	2	3	4	5

Add up the numbers   Total for A =

Interests – group S

I enjoy being with people	1	2	3	4	5
I like to talk things through with people	1	2	3	4	5
I like to pay attention to what people want	1	2	3	4	5
I like helping people	1	2	3	4	5
I like helping people develop and learn things	1	2	3	4	5
Who I am with is more important than where I am	1	2	3	4	5

Add up the numbers   Total for S =

Interests – group E

I enjoy trying to persuade and influence people	1	2	3	4	5
I enjoy using a great deal of energy and resilience	1	2	3	4	5
I like people to do what I ask of them	1	2	3	4	5
I like taking risks	1	2	3	4	5
I like making decisions	1	2	3	4	5
I enjoy getting people organised and excited about doing a task	1	2	3	4	5

Add up the numbers   Total for E =

Interests – group R

	1	2	3	4	5
I like to be given clear directions	1	2	3	4	5
I enjoy getting the details right in my work	1	2	3	4	5
I like a clear structure and regular routine	1	2	3	4	5
I can be relied upon to do what I'm expected to do	1	2	3	4	5
I enjoy working with figures	1	2	3	4	5
I like organising projects, ideas, and people down to the last detail	1	2	3	4	5

Add up the numbers   Total for R =

Enter your scores for each interest group in the boxes below:

P	FO	A	S	E	R

Below are the descriptions of what these letters mean.

[end activity]

Each interest area also links up with one of the main skills areas of DATA, IDEAS, PEOPLE, THINGS.

PRACTICAL INTERESTS: THINGS FOCUS
A high score in PRACTICAL interests indicates you like to work with tools, objects, machines, animals. This would indicate that you like to develop manual, mechanical, agricultural and electronic skills. You might also like building and repairing things and you might like to work with your hands. You tend to admire physical coordination, strength, agility and logic and like to work outdoors and deal with concrete problems. Finally, you prefer to solve problems by DOING.

FINDING OUT INTERESTS: IDEAS FOCUS
A high score in FINDING OUT interests indicates a preference for activities with an investigative focus. You are likely to be curious, studious, independent and sometimes unconventional. You like to develop skills in mathematics, biology and physical sciences and prefer jobs with a scientific or medical focus. You admire logic, use insight, enjoy intellectual challenge. You enjoy solving problems by THINKING them through.

ARTISTIC INTERESTS: IDEAS AND PEOPLE FOCUS
A high score in ARTISTIC interests indicates a preference for activities with an artistic focus. If you score high in this group of interests, language, art, music, drama and writing hold some importance and you tend to be creative, expressive and somewhat independent. You like to be free from routine. You can be non-conformist, sensitive, and introspective. You enjoy being CREATIVE when you solve problems.

SOCIAL INTERESTS: PEOPLE FOCUS
A high score in SOCIAL interests indicates that activities with a people focus are of likely to be of interest to you. You might like activities that involve informing, training, teaching, understanding and helping others. You tend to develop skills for helping others such as those needed by teachers, nurses and counsellors. Because you tend to be helpful, friendly, sensitive, supportive, genuine and empathetic, you like to solve problems by using your FEELINGS.

ENTERPRISING INTERESTS: PEOPLE AND DATA FOCUS
A high score in ENTERPRISING interests indicates that activities involving people and data are likely to be of

interest to you. You might enjoy leading and influencing people and are often outgoing, ambitious, independent, enthusiastic and logical. You are likely to enjoy organising, getting people to work as a team, managing, variety, status, power and money. You like to lead, motivate and persuade people. You typically solve problems by taking RISKS.

ROUTINE INTERESTS: DATA AND THINGS FOCUS
A high score in ROUTINE interests indicates you have a preference for order and clearly defined routines. You probably have an eye for detail. You tend to like order, security and certainty, often identifying with power and status. You probably like developing work systems and utilising new technology. You like organising information in a clear and logical way and you tend to be careful, logical, dependable and accurate and solve problems by following ROUTINES.

Ambitions

You have spent time looking back. The purpose of that reflection and review was to prepare the ground for what you might wish to come next. It will be useful at the end of this section to begin to turn your mind to the future.

Some of us over years store up dreams, ambitions, goals that we lodge at the back of our mind under the heading 'One day I would love to…!'

Some may wish to travel round the world, to climb a mountain, cross a desert, learn to ride a horse, perform in a play or musical and so on. If you have locked away some ambition that you haven't got round to yet, then bring it into the open and consider it again.

It is important for you to look for role models who have achieved their ambitions in the second half of their lives. If possible, talk with them. Ask them how they did it. They might support you in your ambitions. They might advise you on how best to achieve them and alert you to things you might do well to consider. You may find others who just share the dream. Sometimes we admire people from afar and if we do we can ask ourselves what that admiration reflects about our own aspirations and ambitions.

Activity 8

My second half ambitions

Write in your ambitions here:

You will want to revisit these when you get to bringing together all that you have learned about yourself and your world in the final theme.

_____
_____
_____
_____
_____
_____
_____
_____
_____
_____

Continue on next page

_____

_____

_____

_____

_____

_____

_____

_____

_____

_____

_____

_____

_____

_____

_____

_____

[end activity]

Finding out more

We have emphasised the importance of discovering your transferable skills in this theme. A slightly different approach is to focus on what are called 'strengths'. Different people define this in different ways, but an excellent practical and inspirational introduction can be found in a book by Mike Pegg, *The Strengths Way: the art of building on strengths*, Management Books 2000, 2007.

Two more books worth looking at in this area are:

Marcus Buckingham, *Go Put Your Strengths to Work*, Free Press, 2007

Tom Rath, *Strengths Finder*, Gallup Press, 2007

For more information please visit **www.fiftyforward.co.uk**

Summary

You have:

• Explored the concept of ageing and your attitude to it

• Examined your achievements and experiences and your learning from those to apply to your future

• Reflected on the unplanned events that have happened to you and examined what you did to manage and emerge positively from those or what more you might have done

• Kept a record of your use of time and assessed how you might use it better

• Assessed your life values, your transferable skills and your interests

• Noted any ambitions that are still unfulfilled

• Re-visited your life goals and sought support for those.

Action plans

On the basis of your reflections write in what you would like more of, less of and what you would like to keep the same in your life right now.

MORE OF...	LESS OF...	KEEP THE SAME

Choose three that you would like to start working on right now:

1. _____

2. _____

3. _____

> 'I have valued all periods of my life because they have brought me different things. The last 25 years working in my present job have brought great fulfilment – tackling global poverty and injustice – sometimes seeing first hand really desperate poverty and the impact of injustice, oppression and real evil – and then doing day-to-day work to make a difference to the lives of the poorest people and helping them change the world for the better – it doesn't get better than that!'
>
> *Denise, in her 50s*

my work options

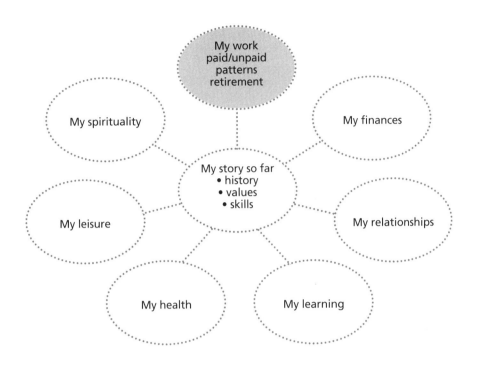

Introduction

Do you work? Of course you do. We all do. So why do some people say that they don't? That may be because we still live with an outdated concept of work, which equates it with employment – work for many still just means having a paid job. In this theme we will seek to challenge that simplistic link, believing it can block a more creative way of looking at our work and our life. Let's be clearer what 'work' can mean.

What is work?

- It is an activity

- It can provide us with a sense of purpose and direction

- It can provide a structure for how we spend our time

- It's where we can learn and develop new skills

- It can give us an identity and self-respect

- It can provide us with friends and a community

- It can influence how other people see and feel about us and how we see and feel about ourselves

- Oh! Yes! And it can in addition provide us with money, if someone wants to buy what we can do.

'And what do *you* do?'

How do you answer that question at social gatherings? For those of us with paid work, talking about our job is how we tend to introduce ourselves and it provides an easy topic to begin a conversation. But how often do we tell people about the other kind of work that we do – unpaid work? It is fairly common for people who have no paid work to suggest, sometimes apologetically, things like, 'I'm retired', 'I'm only a housewife', 'I'm unemployed'.

A number of people who at the time, for various reasons, had no paid work told us,' It is as if in some people's eyes and more importantly in our own eyes we have suddenly become invisible'. The relationship between 'work' and 'worth' is so powerful that when paid work is not part of our lives we can feel less valuable to ourselves, to our family, to our friends, and to the wider society. This is the thinking we need to challenge.

my finances

my relationships

my learning

my health and wellbeing

my leisure

my spirituality

my work options

my finances

my relationships

my learning

my health and wellbeing

my leisure

my spirituality

'There may sometimes be a shortage of jobs but there will never be a shortage of work!'

If you were a teacher when you were employed you will not have lost those teaching skills and you will still be capable of using them in a wide variety of situations. The same applies if you were a sales person, an electrician, a car mechanic, librarian, IT worker, customer service agent, etc.

Why are we more reluctant to tell people about the unpaid work we are doing in our local community, the grandchildren we help to look after, the things we do for our elderly parents, our research into the family's genealogy, etc? And add, 'Oh yes! And I earn my living from working as a sales person at *******'.

The distinction between paid and unpaid work and the implications of the different attitudes to each one is crucial at all times in our lives, but especially when we have passed 50 and begin to run into increased age stereotyping.

We all need work in its widest sense. Without it we might just psychologically wither and die. We do not just want paid work.

This theme has four sections to it.

- **Section 1** focuses on **life values**. In making decisions about paid or unpaid work, or whether or not to retire, it is crucial that we assess what is really important to us – our life values.

- **Section 2** examines **paid work** as the evidence suggests that more of us over 50s want to continue in it for longer and even well past state pension age. You will be asked to assess your transferable skills and your occupational interests and to identify what you are looking for in a job. You can check your scores out against over 700 jobs in 27 job families in the World of Work Map. You can then look up the jobs that might fit for you online at **www.advice-resources.co.uk.** You will also be introduced to a range of flexible working options that are now becoming more realisable, as employers discover that this is the best way to keep or attract valued staff of any age. You will also be able to review some of the myths about older workers.

- **Section 3** will ask you to differentiate between your paid work and your **unpaid work**. For some of us unpaid work will actually be more important than paid work. Those who may not have any paid work currently can explore the possibilities of finding

meaning and satisfaction from unpaid work. Even when we have given up paid work we will always have unpaid work to do.

- **Section 4** re-examines the concept of **retirement** as, along with the concept of unemployment, it did not exist before 1830 and may be coming to the end of its currency. But many people still look forward to some kind of disengagement from paid work and are looking for alternatives to the twentieth century model of full-time employment followed by a sudden transition into no employment – sometimes called 'cliff edge retirement'. New research by Ipsos MORI shows a mixed bag of emotions for those waking up on day one of retirement with under a third saying they felt relaxed and under a quarter feeling free. A surprising one in ten felt anxious, sad or lost.

The following activities will enable you to make best use of the information you now have about your life values.

Section 1: **My life values and work**

This next activity is particularly useful if:

A) You don't have a job and want one

   or

B) You have a job but are actively considering other jobs

Knowing your life values will help you to shape the questions you may want to ask when you get to an interview. Employers generally welcome being asked in depth about the jobs they offer because they too want to ensure that the job you apply for is the right one for you.

You will know your current job well and have some idea whether it reflects your life values. The activity will help you to discover to what extent this is so, or if you may be better off considering alternative jobs.

It may be that your choice of job or career would normally meet most of your key values. However, where you are working and for whom you are working can be the source of dissatisfaction and the cause of problems. Many people leave their jobs because of problems with their line managers; others because of incompatibility with the organisation's culture. In either of these cases, your choice might be to change employers rather than to change career.

Activity 1.1

Does my current job fit with my values?

- Find the table in Appendix 2 that is headed 'My job and my values'. Write in the name of the job (your present job, if you have one) that you wish to check against your life values. Write in the names of any other jobs you are considering.

- Write in the values that you have identified as VERY IMPORTANT and those that you have said are NOT IMPORTANT to you at all.

- Ask yourself to what degree your present (or planned) job satisfies this life value.

  If that value is *never* satisfied by the job, award it 0 points; if that value is *totally* satisfied, award it 10 points. Please use the full range from 0 to 10.

  You will see that a weighting of your answers has already been filled in for you. Simply complete the calculations. For example:

  6 x 8 = 48

  8 x 7 = 56

  2 x 6 = 12 etc.

- Now do the same for any other jobs you might be considering.

- Add up the totals for each job you have analysed.

If you gave ten points for each of your eight VERY IMPORTANT life values your maximum total would be 360 – although it is highly unlikely that anyone would actually achieve 360.

Now answer the following questions for yourself:

my work options

my finances

my relationships

my learning

my health and wellbeing

my leisure

my spirituality

■ How much opportunity is there overall in my current job for me to find expression for my life values?

_____

_____

_____

■ Do any of the values in my NOT IMPORTANT column feature in my present job?

_____

_____

_____

■ Do any of the other jobs that I have analysed more closely fit my key values?

_____

_____

■ How do the jobs compare in the scoring?

_____

_____

■ Does this feel right? If not why not?

_____

_____

_____

■ Do you need additional information before making a choice?[5]

_____

_____

_____

■ Do your answers suggest questions that you might wish to ask at a job interview?

_____

_____

_____

■ Can I think of any objectives that I might want to set myself as a result of this activity?

_____

_____

_____

5 If you know only a little about a job or career you are interested in you can find out more by going to www.advice-resources.co.uk/adviceresources/general where there are over 700 job profiles available. Click on Job Profiles and you will be directed to a list of 27 job families and you can also search according to job titles that you are interested in.

Remember, this will only tell you about the job in general; it will not give you information on the actual job with a particular employer. For that you need to talk with people who work there, look at the company's website or talk directly to the employer.

[end activity]

Activity 1.2

My values and unpaid work

Many people do work for which they receive no payment. They may be caring for their own (or others') children or for an elderly person; they may be working voluntarily in the community or in a myriad of ways.

Unpaid work can provide real satisfaction, especially when the activities reflect our life values, although they may not always coincide.

It is therefore important to consider your unpaid work activities when faced with a choice about whether or not to apply for paid work. Some people may accept a less than ideal job if they get a great deal of satisfaction out of unpaid work.

Reflect on examples of the kind of **unpaid work** that you do in your life. For example: cleaning the house, baby sitting, DIY activities, gardening, church duties, working for a community group or political party, voluntary work, etc.

- In Appendix 2 turn to the table headed 'My unpaid work and my values' and write in the unpaid work activities that you wish to check against your life values.
- Write in your VERY IMPORTANT and your NOT IMPORTANT values again.
- Ask yourself how far this unpaid work activity enables you to satisfy this value. Complete your scoring for each unpaid work activity.

You will see that a weighting of your answers has already been filled in for you. Simply complete the calculations.

After you have completed the scoring, answer the following questions:

■ How do your **unpaid work activities** compare with one another in the scoring?

_____

_____

_____

■ Does this feel right? If not why not?

_____

_____

_____

■ Do any of your **unpaid work activities** contain any of your NOT IMPORTANT values?

_____

_____

_____

■ Do you wish to make any changes as a result of this activity?

_____

_____

_____

[end activity]

> _'The work we do for money must be complemented by the work we do for love…_
> _The menial funds the passion… in old age as much as youth._
> _Some are lucky, (if) the passion pays for itself.'_
>
> Charles Handy 'Age of Enlightenment' Guardian 06/5/06

My values and patterns of employment

Do you know?

- On any given day, 42% of the IBM workforce work in locations away from their base.

- At present over 3.4 million people, about 12% of the working population, work from home either regularly or permanently; this is half a million more than a decade ago.

- From the beginnings of the industrial era, until the end of the twentieth century, the employment options open to everyone were very simple. You could have a 'full-time' job or a 'part-time' job or set up your own business. Full-time work typically involved at least 35 hours a week; part-time work, any number of hours below this. Towards the end of the twentieth century other options began to emerge and in the last few years a plethora of choices have become increasingly available.

- What we do know is that although more and more of the over 50s wish to continue to be employed, they do not just wish for more of the same – in other words, more of 9–5 type jobs. Interestingly, research on 20–30-year-olds is showing the same findings. The most successful companies in the future will be those who offer a wide range of flexible working options.

- A poll carried out by the DTI's _Work Life Balance_ campaign in 2003 found that 46% of job seekers put flexible working as the top benefit they were looking for from their next employer. Seven out of ten wanted to be able to work more flexibly. Sadly, there is evidence that though many people ask for flexibility, it is a minority who are permitted it, especially amongst older (50+) workers, see www.eoc.org.uk and www.eurofound.europa.eu/ewco/studies So what are some of the alternatives now on offer? Please note that these are not mutually exclusive.

- **Traditional 9–5**

  This is still a first choice for many people although as organisations move from hierarchical pyramid structures to project work teams they in turn might prefer a more flexible work force. It is now a work style for only one paid worker out of three.

- **Part time**

  More people are now working part time, especially women. This is particularly useful if help is required for grandchildren or for looking after elderly parents. Many people also prefer it as it gives them time to do other things which are important to them in their lives.

- **Flexitime**

  This is where an agreed number of hours are worked, but when they are worked is open to negotiation. It could be three very long days a week, or annualised hours, or compressed hours, or any combination.

- **Flexiplace**

  This is increasing rapidly as an option. People negotiate how much time they need to spend at the place of employment and how much time they can work from home.

- **Mobile workers (road warriors)**

  This option is increasingly open to sales staff and consultants and is possible simply because of the revolution in new technologies. Mobile phones, laptops, PDA's, satellite navigation, portable printers, podcasts, etc. now enable a genuine work life on the open road. One of the attractions to employers is that no workspace needs to be found.

- **Job sharing**

  Some companies, unhappy about too much part-time work, may feel more at ease with job sharing. The internet now allows people to share jobs around the world. In some IT companies, someone can work for four hours a day in the UK – at which point someone else in the USA, Canada, India or elsewhere may take over.

- **Freelance consultant or contractor**

  This group is primarily self employed; this can be attractive to employers, who do not have to increase their payroll or offer additional benefits. The people doing this have, in theory, huge flexibility as to when and where they work. In practice many of them complain that they often get less time than when they had 9–5 jobs, as they are afraid to say 'no' to a contract offer.

- **Starting up your own business**

  The over 50s do more of this than any other age group. This, and the freelance life, can serve as a bridge to eventual retirement –

although increasing numbers of business owners see themselves doing this until very late old age, dropping their hours as they age.

- **Portfolio workers**

  These people do not want to be restricted to single activities or jobs. They like to have a variety of paid work activities, which they juggle around. Sometimes they like to do similar kinds of work, but with different organisations; in other cases, they like to do totally different kinds of work. We know a media consultant who also owns and runs a market garden business.

- **Home worker**

  This differs from the Flexiplace option as these people wish to work completely from home. Again, the new technologies have provided many paid work options to people who have to be in their homes for a variety of reasons, including health and disability. They also increasingly are setting up their own businesses, run totally from home through the internet or social media. Long gone is the time when this option was a very poorly paid one, demanding little skill or training.

- **Secondments**

  According to the CIPD (Chartered Institute of Personnel Development) secondments are one of the top-ten, most commonly used, career management practices and 67% of respondents considered them to be effective. They can be short term, long term or strategic. The short-term schemes could be just a few months, similar to training programmes that enhance specialist skills, cover busy periods or complete special projects. A long-term secondment might be for around 12 months to a couple of years and have a different set of objectives, for the secondee and the organisation. Strategic secondments could help to foster relationships with other businesses or countries deemed important for commercial success for the seconding organisation. Increasing numbers of employees are requesting, and getting, career breaks to raise families, travel the world or to pursue a dream.

In addition, you may also be attracted to organisations that allow career breaks and even sabbaticals.

6 CIPD Factsheet on Secondment 2008.

my work options

my finances

my relationships

my learning

my health and wellbeing

my leisure

my spirituality

my work options

my finances

my relationships

my learning

my health and wellbeing

my leisure

my spirituality

> '*In spite of the misused phrase 'work–life balance', work is not the opposite of life, but is at its core, provided that it is work that one enjoys and that can be done at a pace that suits. What many more accurately want is not more life and less work but a better balance of the different types of work. The work we do for money needs to be complemented by the work we do for love or duty, in the home or in the community, as well as by the work we do for pleasure and the work we do to improve our skills and knowledge.*'
>
> Charles Handy 'Age of Enlightenment' The Guardian, 06/05/06

> '*Already a quarter of the workforce is part time and another quarter are self-employed or in tiny 1 to 4 person businesses, most of them working that way from choice but others because they have to, particularly as they age.*'
>
> Ibid

Activity 1.3

My values and patterns of employment

Ask yourself which of these employment patterns hold most attraction for you. If you are already employed you may wish to compare what you currently have, to other patterns that you may not have considered or now wish to consider.

Turn to Appendix 2 and find the table headed 'Patterns of employment and my values'

Write in your VERY IMPORTANT and your NOT IMPORTANT values again.

Ask yourself the question: "How far would this pattern of employment enable me to satisfy this value?" Complete your scoring for each employment pattern.
You will see that a weighting of your answers has already been filled in for you. Simply complete the calculations.

Answer the following questions:

■ How do the employment patterns compare in the scoring?

_____

_____

_____

■ Does this feel right? If not why not?

_____

_____

_____

■ Do any of the patterns you are considering contain any of your NOT IMPORTANT values?

_____

_____

_____

■ Do you need additional information before making a choice?

_____

_____

_____

■ Do your answers suggest questions that you might wish to ask at a career development or a job interview?

_____

_____

_____

■ Do you need to set yourself any objectives?

_____

_____

_____

[end activity]

my work options

my finances

my relationships

my learning

my health and wellbeing

my leisure

my spirituality

my work options

my finances

my relationships

my learning

my health and wellbeing

my leisure

my spirituality

Section 2: **My paid work**

Do you know?

- Age Concern has estimated that annual economic output could rise by as much as £29.7 billion if nearly one million older adults rejoined the workforce (Age Concern, 2004), leaving aside the additional, but hidden, costs of poorer health in inactive older people.

- An increasing number of people are choosing to remain in work beyond pensionable age: 6% in 1997 and 8% in 2004. The CIPD state that in 2008 that figure has increased to 11% and their latest research suggests that up to 40% of 50–64-year-olds plan to work beyond State Pension Age (SPA).

- 71% of those aged between 50 and SPA are in employment, compared to 82% of those aged 25–49 and 59% of those aged 16–24.

- B&Q's Macclesfield store, staffed entirely by people over age 50, achieved 18% more profit, 39% less absenteeism and 59% less shrinkage than benchmarked stores (B&Q).

- Nationwide Building Society saved £7 million in staff turnover costs by extending the recruitment age to 60+.

- Halifax Building Society increased profits by £130,000 at six branches, trialing an older workforce.

- Small and medium-sized businesses (over 90% of all businesses) show less age discrimination than larger hierarchical businesses, so maybe they are the best targets for 50+ job hunting.

- People over 50 without paid work are 50% more likely to die of respiratory diseases and experience depressive disorders than those in paid work, and three times more likely to visit the doctor. They are also less likely to participate in other activities including volunteering, caring and learning.

- A recent report reveals that 70% of employers are looking to recruit over 55s, while 31% are actively hiring people who are already of pensionable age. ('Recruitment, Retention and Turnover Survey' CIPD annual report, 2006.)

- William Bridges states that the lack of job security in today's workplace means that we are all temporary workers and that 'all jobs in today's economy are temporary'.

- Self-employment is more common among older workers than among those under 50. In spring 2004, 19% of people aged 50 and over in the UK were self-employed compared with 14% of people aged 25–49. Self-employment was also more common in older men than older women (26% compared with 11% respectively).

- 72% of men and 68% of women between 50 and SPA were employed in 2004, compared with 64% and 60% in 1994. The Government has a target of 80%.

- Official statistics show men over 65 and women over 60 are the fastest-growing group in the workforce.

- There are now 6.6 million men aged between 50 and 64 and women aged 50 to 59, working in the UK. This is more than the number of 25–34-year-olds in jobs.

- In a survey published in 2008 by the DWP of over 1,000 people aged 55+ on attitudes to work and retirement :

  - 63% said they were continuing to work on for financial reasons

  - 57% wanted to work because they enjoyed their jobs

  - 38% because their job helped keep their mind active

  - 32% because they didn't feel old enough to stop working

  - 31% because they would miss it if they stopped working

  - 23% because they believed their job kept them fit and healthy

  - 18% because they worried they would be bored if they stopped working.

- 'Skills Envy Sweeps the Nation'. Forget beauty or money – the real thing we envy in others is their skills, according to a poll commissioned by the Learning and Skills Council (LSC) in 2007. More than a third of respondents confessed to envying the skills and abilities of others, whereas only 4% felt jealous of other people's beauty. The survey marked the launch of a new campaign, Our Future, aimed at inspiring people and business to improve their skill levels and ultimately support the target set by Lord Leitch, in his review of skills for the UK, to become a world leader in all levels of skills by 2020. Many respondents also saw skills as playing an integral part in feeling in control of their lives:

- 90% of respondents believe they have the ability to control their future using current skills or by learning new ones.

- 47% people felt that access to training to improve their skills would help them feel more in control of their lives.

- Millions of British workers are still dreaming about what they want to do 'when they grow up'... and they're aged over 50! Forty-six per cent of those who are 50+ say they are not too old to start a new career or fulfil lifetime job goals, according to major new research by learndirect Careers Advice.

- Age is not stopping one in five workers who are less than a decade away from retirement seriously contemplating a career change to fulfil a lifetime job ambition. More than a quarter of this group also admit they want more job satisfaction in their next career move – and for them that means doing something 'more worthwhile'. In fact, 61% want the chance to learn new skills.

What are companies doing?

Nationwide extended the upper age limit for retirement to 75; 14% of employees are aged 50+ (compared to 8.6% in 2001 and less than 1% in 1980s). Within this group, 15.23% are aged 60+, which equates to 1.83% of total employee population. The oldest Branch Manager is aged 61. The oldest employee is 74. Nationwide has a pre-interview screening process, which does not assess applicants on age but on competence.

The **Co-operative Society** has abandoned any formal retirement ages and more and more companies, especially SMEs are doing this.

IBM keeps reserves of retired workers for when they need additional help. They also have an innovative flexible retirement programme through which people, up to three years prior to an agreed retirement date, can work fewer hours and begin to take a portion of their pensions.

Asda has two key groups of workers – young people, often students wanting to work in holiday time, and older people who want to work in holiday time, often because it is too expensive to take holidays at this peak time. These workers are on a contract but only have to work ten weeks a year during holiday times. Asda employs 8,000 permanent temps who work for ten weeks a year. This should cut down their £2.6 million recruitment budget. They have pensioner days and 'bring your granny to work' days, carer's leave, grandparent's leave, Benidorm leave – for people who would like to spend some winter months in Spain or some other sunny clime. Asda is also looking at ways in which its older recruits might work their way up to management level. It is the largest employer of over 50s. Carer's leave can be up to three months off.

B&Q was delighted to receive the 'Age-Positive Retailer of the Year' award in the People in Retail Awards in 2006. Garden centre customer advisor, Sydney Prior aged 92, collected the award on behalf of B&Q, thanking his store manager for giving him the opportunity to join the company at the age of 75. Sydney joined the Wimbledon store after retiring and is B&Q's oldest employee. Sydney comments: 'Working at B&Q gives me the chance to put my knowledge and experience to good use, advising customers on their gardening projects. On top of that, working with people of all ages gives youngsters the chance to learn a little from an old timer like myself, and they help to keep me young at heart!' With a total workforce of 38,000, nearly 25% of B&Q staff are over the age of 50, effectively balanced with 20% of staff being under the age of 24.

BT say 'Mixed-age teams provide us with the best opportunity to truly understand our customers' needs and reap the benefits of the rich diversity of views, opinions and experiences.' Older workers are also requesting flexible working: 'Since age legislation came into place, we found that 80% of older workers (60+) wanted to work on.'

Businesses who have taken steps to tackle age-related issues report a number of large-scale benefits including:

• Improved staff retention rates, higher morale, higher productivity, fewer short-term absences, a better public image, access to a wider customer base and retention of a wider range of skills and experience.

• An additional benefit is that mature workers make excellent mentors. Many highly skilled older workers

my work options

my finances

my relationships

my learning

my health and wellbeing

my leisure

my spirituality

my work options

my finances

my relationships

my learning

my health and wellbeing

my leisure

my spirituality

still retire completely and abruptly, taking with them valuable skills and knowledge which companies have done little to extract from them or encourage them to pass on. Developing older workers as mentors and vehicles for succession planning not only addresses this problem, but provides jaded older employees with new impetus to continue.

Transferable skills

You're more skilled than you think

Traditionally, we underestimate our skills and abilities. Often this is because we only think in job specific terms. Let's look at an example. A waiter, when asked what skills he has, might reply, 'none – I'm just a waiter'. He doesn't feel he has any skills to speak of, because he is unable to see deeper than what he does every day.

Below is an example of the transferable skills that underpin his job and might be applied to other jobs.

The following table shows how wrong he is to say 'I am only a waiter'.

JOB CONTENT SKILL	Working with data	Working with people	Working with ideas	Working with things
seating people	assessing which tables can take the numbers of people entering	making people feel welcome	reviewing table layout	manipulating items rapidly
suggesting menu items	ability to memorise items	being persuasive	thinking of new menu possibilities from listening to people's comments	
taking orders	explaining menu items – writing clearly to be understood by others	helping people to understand the options and to make decisions	thinking of alternatives to help customers with their choices	learning to use new computerised ordering and billing system
delivering orders to kitchen	communicating information to others and having good knowledge of food	checking for understanding; maintaining relationships	thinking of new systems for dealing with orders	operating and monitoring the ordering system
serving food	remembering who ordered what	remembering who is to get which order	suggestions for improving presentation of some dishes	manual dexterity; avoiding spillage whilst balancing items
checking on satisfaction	seeking feedback	listening and caring, and ability to maintain service under pressure	thinking of new ways of getting customer feedback	
delivering bill, taking money and providing change	Numeracy	dealing with people courteously		operating tills or handheld computers
thanking them		dealing with people courteously, organising a smooth exit with coats returned and no items left		

We can see from this example that the waiter is, in fact, very skilled. He just needed to look beyond his job for the underlying skills which could in fact be transferred to many other jobs.

Activity 1.4

My transferable skills

Take some time to think about your own skills. Remember, they do not have to be related only to paid work. Examine what you do to be successful in life generally and particularly in unpaid work. Here are a few examples of non-job-related skills to give you some ideas.

- Skills involved in organising and preparing dinner for six people

- Assembling and fitting a new wardrobe

- Managing a household budget – balancing the books, dealing with household bills, planning for future expenditure

- Laying out and planting a garden

- Being a supportive friend, through good times and tough times.

■ Can you produce some examples of your own that relate to unpaid work?

_____

_____

_____

[end activity]

We need to realise that:

- We all have skills that equip us to do a range of jobs

- We should not limit or define ourselves by our current or previous jobs

- Many skills are transferable across other jobs

- Just because we are competent in a job doesn't mean we will be motivated to do it

- As we do a job, and as we age, we grow and develop; if our job doesn't change we will outgrow it. There will be less challenge in it for us – we can do it 'in our sleep'. That may be just the point to take our skills and experience and head in another direction!

Activity 6 enabled you to list your most transferable skills. Remind yourself what they are.

The World of Work Map

This map (overleaf) contains over 700 jobs, classified into 27 'job families'. A 'job family' is a group of jobs related to one another on the basis of their focus in working with data, ideas, people and things. The map is split into 12 regions.

- Those regions next to each other have the most in common.

- Those on opposite sides have least in common.

You can see the regions of the maps that your transferable skills and your work interests point towards.

To find out more about a particular job go online to **www.advice-resources.co.uk/adviceresources/general**. In the box that says 'find a resource', use the drop-down menu to where it says 'job profiles'. Click on 'go'. This will take you to a page headed 'job profiles'. Where it says, 'start using the resource: job profiles', click on 'job profiles'. This will take you to the list of 27 job families. If you wish to explore a job and are unsure which family it is in simply type in the name of the job into the Career Keyword Search and you will be directed straight to it.

You will find a full description of the work, its requirements, the hours and environment, the skills and interests you will need, entry requirements, training needed, opportunities for employment, likely annual income, and many references for further information.

my work options
my finances
my relationships
my learning
my health and wellbeing
my leisure
my spirituality

World of Work Map

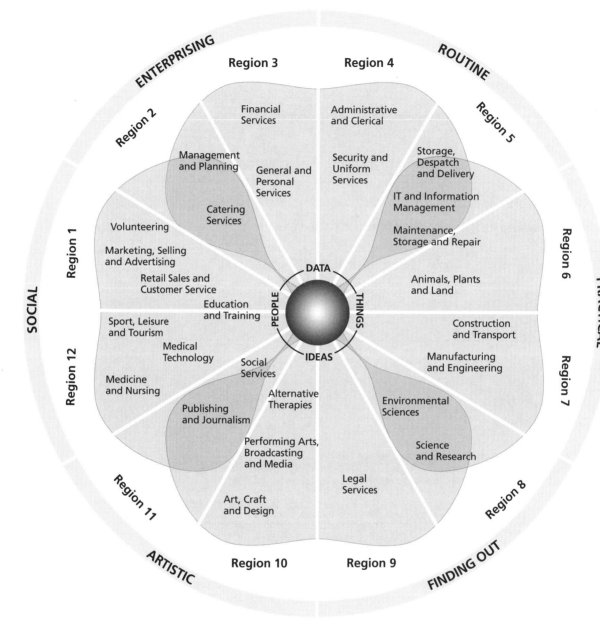

If you would like to discuss your career options with a learning advisor at the learndirect advice line, call 0800 100 900 or use the online enquiry form.

If you have transferable skills primarily in:

PEOPLE – you might want to explore jobs in — Regions 12 & 1
PEOPLE AND DATA – you might want to explore jobs in — Region 2

DATA – you might want to explore jobs in — Regions 3 & 4
DATA AND THINGS – you might want to explore jobs in — Region5

THINGS – you might want to explore jobs in — Regions 6 & 7
THINGS AND IDEAS – you might want to explore jobs in — Region 8

IDEAS – you might want to explore jobs in — Regions 9 & 10
IDEAS AND PEOPLE – you might want to explore jobs in — Region 11

■ Ask yourself: "What do I realise after identifying my most transferable skills and those I do not wish to use?"

_____

_____

_____

_____

Activity 1.5

What are my work interests?

In Theme 1, My Work Options, you were able to assess your work interests by completing Activity 7. Looking at the 'world of work' map you can also see the job regions and job families your work interests might lead you to.

You will see that each interest type corresponds to two regions.

PRACTICAL	=	Regions 6 and 7
FINDING OUT	=	Regions 8 and 9
ARTISTIC	=	Regions 10 and 11
SOCIAL	=	Regions 12 and 1
ENTERPRISING	=	Regions 2 and 3
ROUTINE	=	Regions 4 and 5

Ask yourself the following questions:

■ Am I surprised at my interest scores? If so in what way?

_____

_____

_____

_____

■ Have I chosen paid work that has matched my interests over the years? If so what have been the consequences? If my interests have not matched my paid work, what have been the consequences of that?

_____

_____

_____

_____

■ What unpaid work might satisfy someone with my interests?

_____

_____

_____

_____

[end activity]

my finances

my relationships

my learning

my health and wellbeing

my leisure

my spirituality

Activity 1.6

Myths and facts about older workers

Below are some statements that are often made about older workers. Tick according to whether you think that each one is true or false.

1. Older workers are less productive.   true ☐   false ☐

2. Older workers take off more sick time.   true ☐   false ☐

3. Older workers are less competent.   true ☐   false ☐

4. Older workers are less capable of making decisions and evaluating information.   true ☐   false ☐

5. Older workers are less adaptable and don't learn as well.   true ☐   false ☐

6. Small businesses started by people aged 50+ are twice as likely to succeed as businesses started by younger people.   true ☐   false ☐

7. 40% of the newly created jobs in the past year have been filled by people over pensionable age.   true ☐   false ☐

8. Men in their 50s who are self-employed are much more likely than those who are employees to still be working ten years later.   true ☐   false ☐

9. Older workers are more uncomfortable with new technologies.   true ☐   false ☐

[end activity]

Here are the correct answers:

1. False – data from the UK and the USA states that employees in their late 50s and 60s are more conscientious and hard working than younger workers.

2. False – sickness absence is highest in the 16–24 age group (3.2%) and stays constant from age 35 to SPA (2.8%). It is lowest amongst workers over SPA.

3. False – the average age for top jobs in all sectors has increased steadily over the past 15 years.

4. False – studies show that older employees are actually more capable of evaluating decisions than younger ones. However, they usually take longer because experience has taught them the wisdom of caution.

5. False – people who stay engaged in life continue to adapt and learn. California State University compared the marks of students aged 18–25 and those aged 49–72. There were no significant differences between them. In fact the only difference was that the older people completed training at a significantly higher rate.

6. True – in addition, self-employment is the second most popular option among the 'Never Retire' group.

Over 17% of older workers between 50 and State Pension Age (SPA) are self-employed, compared with 12% of those aged 25–49 and less than 4% of those aged 16–24 (DWP, 2006).

7. True – according to the latest data from the Office of National Statistics (2007).

8. True – and in addition, workers over SPA were more likely to be employed in small companies with up to 10 staff – and far less likely to be employed in larger organisations with over 50 staff.

9. False – no longer the domain of only the young, the internet is fast becoming the 'hip hangout' for older generations. A survey conducted in 2007 by the internet research firm Hitwise UK revealed that any day now, silver surfers (classified as internet users aged 55 and over) look likely to overtake the 35–44 age group as the one with the largest representation online. During a four-week period in 2007, those aged 55+ accounted for 22% of UK visits to all types of websites. Those aged 35–44 only just pipped them to the post, at 23.5%.

How well did you do?

Section 3: **My unpaid work**

my work options

my finances

my relationships

my learning

my health and wellbeing

my leisure

my spirituality

Do you know?

- The value of unpaid support that carers provide has now reached £87 billion a year, according to a new report published in September 2007 by Carers UK – more than the annual total spend on the NHS, which stood at nearly £82 billion in the year 2006–7. The average carer is saving the nation over £15,260 a year. The new figures are also more than four times the amount spent on social care services for adults and children by local authorities each year – £19.3 billion in the year 2005–6.

- In the UK, the over 60s contribute around 18 million hours of voluntary work per week, or approximately 792 million hours per year. At the UK's current minimum wage their work is worth over £4 billion each year.

- People aged 50–74 are more likely to do voluntary work than younger adults. A study in 2006 showed that the majority of older citizens engaged on average in 11 different activities and spent nearly 20 hours a week in community organisations.

'I have come to realise that work is something that is important in itself, rather than a necessary way to earn a living. Work brings its own fulfilment and in a way is crucial to being human. It is part of being creative, hence why unemployment is such a curse. People are more important than money. God created the world as 'good' so it is important to be positive, hopeful and trusting. Wisdom is a most precious gift, but it takes time to acquire it – there are no short cuts. Anything really worth having has to be worked for.'

Denise, in her 50s

Most of us at some point will cease paid work either by choice or necessity. When this happens it will be valuable for us to find other ways of using these skills. Even if you are in full-time paid work right now it is useful preparation to begin to think of what you can choose to do.

Activity 1.7

My unpaid work

Think of all of the work that you do which is unpaid – at home, for the family, in voluntary groups, your hobbies, social activities, etc. Some people find it difficult to value unpaid work, which can often involve using as many skills as those needed for paid work. If you are considering re-entering the world of paid work, it is useful to have examples of voluntary work to talk and write about, which demonstrate your underlying transferable skills and their application to the benefit of the community.

Look at your list of most transferable skills compiled earlier on. These are the skills or strengths that, when you use them, make you feel most fulfilled. This is work that hardly feels like work. You are energised, passionate, 'in the zone' as some sports people call it.

Rank them in terms of how important it is for you to be able to apply these skills.

■ Now take them in order and write in any ideas you may have as to how you could utilise each of these skills in unpaid work.

_____

_____

_____

_____

'Getting people to talk', for example. You could use this in a social club, voluntary work with young or old people, in a church study group, travelling with a group, in a teaching situation where you are teaching others about something of which you have specialist knowledge – car maintenance, using the internet, playing a card game, cooking, gardening, etc.

See how many ideas you can come up for using your most transferable skills.

Transferable skill	How I use it now	How else I might use it
1.		
2.		
3.		
4.		
5.		
6.		
7.		
8.		
9.		

[end activity]

> 'I was a member of the British Red Cross Society for many years working with disabled young adults. I was part of a group that set up and ran a 10 day long Victorian festival which has now been going for 20 years. I was a member of the steering group responsible for getting a new theatre built in our town. I held various positions including Vice-Chair and Treasurer of 'Channel Arts Association' which organised the annual National Youth Arts Festival in Devon for a number of years. Currently I help organise the annual North Devon Festival of Choirs, mainly responsible for publicity and programming'.
>
> *Janet in her 60s*

Section 4: **My retirement**

my work options

my finances

my relationships

my learning

my health and wellbeing

my leisure

my spirituality

Retirement is the point at which a person stops full-time paid work completely. A person may also semi-retire and keep some sort of job, although usually out of choice rather than necessity.

In most countries, the idea of a fixed retirement age is of recent origin, being introduced during the nineteenth and twentieth centuries. Before then, the absence of pension arrangements meant that most workers continued to work until death or illness stopped them. They then relied on personal savings or the support of family or friends. Nowadays most developed nations have systems to provide pensions on retirement which may be self-financed or funded by employers or the state; but as we shall see, ideas about and attitudes to retirement are rapidly changing.

'I do not think my parents looked forward to retirement as it was one step away from the grave. I was lucky; education enabled me to have a broader view of the world.'

Bodger, in his 60s

Retirement as permanent separation from the workplace is being replaced for some with the idea of 'bridge employment'. Bridging is a form of partial retirement in which an older worker alternates periods of disengagement from the workplace with periods of temporary, part-time, occasional, self-employed work and any variations of the different patterns of employment described on pages 52–3. Bridging allows older workers to 'practise' retirement, to fill labour market shortages, or to try a variety of occupational positions after an initial period of retirement. A two-year project by the CIPD and Tomorrow People, the Opportunity of a Lifetime: Reshaping Retirement questions the government's approach of 'delayed retirement' and instead calls for 'liquid lives'.

Retirement should no longer be a distinct phase of life. People need to mix and match work and extend leisure and learning throughout their lives, while traditional approaches to career development also need to change.

Rather than being stuck in an unfulfilling career by the fear of impending retirement, people need to feel able to change career into their fifties and beyond, the report states, while an increased supply of older workers mean they are looked on in a more positive light. Bridging is sometimes described as a second career. The American Association of Retired Persons received 36,000 responses to a working life survey, covering 375 job titles from workers age 50+, who had returned to the workplace after an initial period of retirement. The three most frequently cited reasons for returning included having financial need, liking to work, and keeping busy. However, closer examination of the data revealed that 'financial need' included money to help adult children as well as to meet basic needs. 'Liking to work' included feeling successful, enjoying the excitement of the workplace, and making a contribution. 'Keeping busy' included working with a spouse, staying healthy, or fulfilling a social need. Reasons cited for remaining or returning to the workplace expressed the social meaning of work. Work is more than earning a living. It is a way to live.

'You never retire from your vocation… and so I will continue to work while I can.'

Mike Pegg, in his 60s

The traditional notion of retirement may be replaced for many with lifelong working – in various positions and in varying amounts of time throughout adult life. Retirement, the end stage of a linear working life, may be replaced by a learning, working, leisure, working, learning, life cycle.

In such a cyclical living and working model, participating in the work force never ceases, but is interspersed with periods of leisure and learning. Full-time work may be interspersed with periods of flexible working arrangements, such as part-time, seasonal, occasional, and project work.

'I retired at 65 in 1991 and as I was still fairly fit took some part-time jobs nearly immediately. As I have always been interested in development issues I took a job with the DEC (Development Education Centre) which

my work options

my finances

my relationships

my learning

my health and wellbeing

my leisure

my spirituality

deals with these problems at every level; personal, social, community. I also joined a group trying to give some support to people having a drink problem. With a group of friends we started a Credit Union for the local community, which after 10 years amalgamated with the much bigger Leeds City Credit Union. I have been retired for 16 years now and it has been a mostly enjoyable time, but it is not without its drawbacks. The main one is that overnight the structure of your days has been pulled down. While work was giving a rhythm to your day, when you stop work you have to find everyday a new structure for your day. This is destabilising and the same applies to the whole year. When you are in work you have holidays to look forward to but when you retire, paradoxically you lose your holidays!'

Guy, in his 80s

Do you know?

- Six in ten people define the word 'retirement' as some combination of work and leisure.

- In a global study those still in full-time paid work expect to continue working rather than retiring early. 71% say it is because they want to. Of those over 60s who had continued working for as long as possible, 67% say they did so because they wanted to.

- There is evidence that many who retired early and found nothing to replace their paid work have regretted it; and that subsequent generations are slowly beginning to reject it as desirable.

- The same survey shows that, far from being a time of misery, penury and frailty, life for most people in their 60s and 70s is characterised by good health, independence, control and a good quality of life.

- Malcolm Forbes famously said, 'Retirement kills more people than hard work ever did.'

- A 26-year study of more than 3,500 former employees of Shell in Texas has found that men and women who retired at 55 were nearly twice as likely to die within the following ten years as those who retired at 60 or 65. The research by Shan Tsai of Shell Health Services in Houston, explodes the myth that early retirement leads to a longer life expectancy. 'Although some workers retired at 55 because of failing health, these results clearly show that early retirement is not associated with

increased survival,' Tsai said in the study. 'On the contrary, mortality improved with increasing age at retirement for people from both high and low socio-economic groups.'

- A recent study by insurer GE Life has estimated that 10% of retired people now work part-time for an average of 14 hours per week to supplement their income.

- The higher the level of qualification an older person has attained, the greater the probability of them being in employment. In 2004, 81% of people aged between 50 and State Pension Age (SPA), with a degree, were in employment, compared with 74% of people with the equivalent of GCSEs and 52% of people with no qualifications. The trend is similar for both men and women.

- The fear of not being able to cope financially after retirement is felt by only a relatively small proportion of pre-retirees, and the same is true for post-retirees. 70% of pre-and post-retirees are not worried.

- Over a third of people aged 50–69 in Great Britain who have retired considered that they were forced into retirement. Health problems were the most common reason for those forced to retire before SPA. People in this group were more likely to have no formal qualifications and much less likely to have an income from a private pension, compared with those who retired voluntarily.

- A study from the Centre for Research into the Older Workforce (CROW), at the University of Surrey, showed that those with higher qualifications and income – and those in professional and managerial jobs – have more positive experiences of work, and are more likely to remain in work into their late 50s and beyond. Those without qualifications, on low incomes and in routine occupations are more likely to be squeezed out in their 50s. The survey found that older workers (78%) would be willing to consider work of some sort after they formally retire. Over half would consider part-time or occasional work, and a third would consider voluntary work. However, fewer than one in ten would consider full-time work.

Moving on from paid work

In companies that embark on 'downsizing', the people who face most difficulty in coming to terms with and moving on from job loss are those who thought they had a 'secure job' and had never contemplated an alternative. While stunned with thoughts of 'why me?', and the pain and hurt of feeling rejected, they have to collect themselves and start again.

For those being made redundant, or those facing a retirement that they haven't chosen, it can be valuable to face the question:

'When I leave my job, what will I be losing that I have now?'

Typical answers include:

- Income
- A place to go every day
- A reason to get out of bed
- A structure to our time, our days and our life
- Opportunity to meet people
- Friendships
- Respect in the eyes of our family, friends and neighbours
- A chance to use our skills
- A chance to learn new things
- Pride and a belief in ourselves
- A sense of importance and achievement
- Work that we love.

What is interesting about this list of losses is how closely they relate to the concept of 'needs' as identified by the psychologist Abraham Maslow. In our working lives we typically put most of our 'eggs into the one basket'. We seek to answer the vast majority of our needs through the channel of our job. That can be rewarding, but it can also be high risk. Somebody, or some organisation, can take that basket away and yet we still have the same needs.

In his study of 'normal' (as distinct from dysfunctional) people and their reasons for choosing to work rather than be idle, Maslow identified that we work to provide for our 'needs'. He identified that we have needs that move through a hierarchy.[7]

Basically, Maslow says, we work to provide food and shelter for ourselves and those we love. If those needs are satisfied, we work to satisfy higher needs; to have a secure environment, to be free from threat and fear. When those needs are satisfied we are still not likely to sit back. We then need to have pride in ourselves and recognition from others. Then we like to work to use all our talents, to be all we are capable of being, and so on.

Our progress up Maslow's hierarchy is not all one way. At different times in our lives we will be working for higher needs than others. When our jobs are taken away we can slide down the pyramid and go back to the basics of finding new ways to pay our mortgage and the bills. That urge can be so urgent that frequently people in that position take the first job available. They are earning again, but are in a job that does not provide for their other needs. They have to climb again.

When we face redundancy or enforced retirement we are facing the loss of what has been the major way of having our needs met.

In an age when no job, in whatever organisation, or at whatever level is secure, then our security comes from:

- always having an alternative
- never being too single-tracked
- not putting all our eggs in the one basket.

7 Source of diagram www.deepermind.com.htm

my finances

my relationships

my learning

my health and wellbeing

my leisure

my spirituality

Activity 1.8

Moving on from paid work

Can you imagine ways in which, if you were made redundant or retired, you could have your needs met?

In what ways, apart from a full-time job, could you:

■ Sell your skills or experience to earn some income?

_____

_____

_____

_____

■ Structure your time to give your days order and purpose?

_____

_____

_____

_____

■ Contribute your skills to worthwhile groups/causes?

_____

_____

_____

_____

■ Be involved with other people?

_____

_____

_____

_____

■ Be involved in things that maintain pride in yourself and respect from others?

_____

_____

_____

_____

my work options

my finances

my relationships

my learning

my health and wellbeing

my leisure

my spirituality

■ Maintain or enhance your standing in the eyes of others?

_____

_____

_____

_____

■ Learn new skills or develop new expertise?

_____

_____

_____

_____

■ Start or be involved in projects or activities that will give you a sense of achievement and fulfilment?

_____

_____

_____

_____

People carrying these questions into retirement are beginning now to design portfolio lives, which comprise some paid work, some voluntary work, some learning and development, some involvement in projects with other retirees, some engagement with grandchildren, some new hobbies or interests (See Theme 6 on Leisure) and so on, and are building lives that can be as satisfying as any previous paid work phase.

Note also – the list of things that people said they had lost when their jobs disappeared was not entirely negative. Some also said they were happy about losing:

- A very stressful job
- A boss who was a total pain
- Long hours and days away from home
- Hours spent on motorways and in traffic jams
- Colleagues who bored you to tears or were annoying in one way or another
- Customers who were never happy, etc.

Not every job is a delight or a complete answer to our needs!

You could start a chat room (see **www.fiftyforward.co.uk**) to exchange ideas with others who have faced the challenges identified here and found ways, without having a full-time job, of meeting the needs discussed above!

[end activity]

Activity 1.9

So what has retirement ever done for you or might do for you?

Please answer the questions in Column A, if you have stopped all paid work – or the questions in Column B, if you still do some paid work.

COLUMN A I have stopped all paid work	COLUMN B I still do some paid work
At what age?	How many hours a week?
What do I miss?	Why do I do it? - income - nature of the work - structure - new learning - friendship - status - contributing something of value (rank order)
What have I gained?	What don't I like about doing it?
What unpaid work am I doing?	How long might I continue with paid work?
Why do I like doing this? - nature of the work - structure - new learning - friendship - status - contributing something of value (rank order)	

■ Am I satisfied with having given up all paid work and why?

_____

_____

_____

■ Am I pleased that I still have some paid work and why?

_____

_____

_____

[end activity]

my work options

my finances

my relationships

my learning

my health and wellbeing

my leisure

my spirituality

> *'..retirement is a great opportunity to develop latent capacities and gifts and perhaps to meet one's own needs in a way not possible before. Learning to live with more freedom of choice and with more available time can be anxiety provoking and even depressing, as well as exciting and desirable.'*
>
> *Janet in her 60s*

If you are currently in full- or part-time employment, these are some of the options you might consider:

- Retire but continue to work for the same employer but in a reduced capacity
- Partially retire and work part time for a different employer
- Job share
- Work as a consultant or freelancer for a former employer
- Start a business
- Short-term contract with same employer
- Home working
- Portfolio working – where you will have two or more jobs with different employers.

If we find our paid work satisfying, or if we need paid work to fund our chosen lifestyle, then retirement will not be amongst our plans. But for some, the idea of retirement at the end of a long working life can seem like a 'promised land', a reward for many years of commitment and dedicated work. Indeed, for many of us, retirement (some have called it 'freetirement') will have to be faced at some stage, as opportunities for paid work begin to dry up. Whether chosen or enforced, retirement is a key stage for many in our lives and careers.

It was always interesting on the workshops we ran to ask people 'If your income were guaranteed how much of what you do with your life would you continue to do?' There were very few who said they would continue to work as hard or as long as they were doing, and there were many who said 'It would be great to have that choice!'

As we age, we are likely to become conscious that we will not 'go on forever'. We may have 'worked to live, and not lived to work!' Our work may have given us many things, it may have supported us and our families, it may have helped us grow and learn, it may have provided for our needs and interests, but if we have a choice…?

Robert Atchley,[8] when exploring the process of ageing, suggests that as we age we engage with a psychological process called 'continuity'. This amounts to an ability in the older person to maintain a 'strong sense of purpose and self in the face of the changes associated with ageing'. 'Continuity' helps us to 'evolve psychologically and socially' and cope with life events such as retirement, loss of a partner or increasing physical disability. Atchley's work suggests that though there are physical, psychological and social challenges as a consequence of ageing, most of us cope well and find considerable satisfaction in our later years.

Atchley also suggested there are phases in the process of retirement.

- **'Pre-retirement phase'**;[9] we become aware that retirement lies ahead for us, it may be years ahead but it is going to happen; we look to our finances, begin to dream of things we would like to do and prepare ourselves for the change.

- **'Honeymoon phase'**; retirement happens, we enjoy the free time; we do all the jobs we never had time to do and all the things we had promised ourselves 'one day'.

- **'Disenchantment phase'**; a re-questioning of how attractive retirement actually is; when we have done all we planned what else is there to do? We can begin to feel depressed about life and tired, though we have time on our hands.

- **'Reorientation phase'**; we re-assess ourselves and our situation; we become more realistic about how we will use our time; we re-evaluate the options open to us (perhaps in paid or unpaid work, in learning, in leisure or social activities). We identify our priorities and make decisions that will move us on to the next stage.

- **'Stability phase'**; we establish a routine of activities we have chosen and pursue them happily; we begin to feel competent, important and happy again.

- **'Terminal phase'**; we may eventually arrive at a stage where our declining health or resources begins to reduce our options and we begin to wind down and accept new boundaries; though, as our generations become increasingly healthy and longer living, this phase is likely to be greatly delayed. Indeed, for some it may be termed the 'terminal phase' because they put an end to retirement by returning to paid work!

8 *Continuity and Adaptation in Aging: Creating Positive Experiences*, Robert Atchley, Johns Hopkins University Press, USA 1999.
9 The later material on Life Transitions presents a generic model of transition stages which approximate very closely to this research.

Activity 1.10

Planning for retirement

So here are some questions and matters for reflection when facing the prospect of retirement.

How much is enough?

Theme 2, Finance, looks at the relationship between our income and expenditure and we consider our assets. Alongside that picture we need to consider, without being morbid, how long we think we might live. Looking at our family patterns of longevity, looking at how healthy our lifestyle is, looking at life expectancy for someone of our gender and our age how long might we have left? (In the UK men aged 65 can expect to live at least a further 16.6 years and women a further 19.4 years if mortality rates remained the same as they were in 2003–05, **www.statistics.gov.uk**.) We can then consider questions such as:

- How long might I need paid work?
- What lifestyle will I aspire to in retirement?
- What lifestyle will I be able to afford in my retirement?
- How can I best use my assets to give me more options at that stage?
- What might I need to put aside in case things don't work out?
- Do I want to leave any financial legacy to anybody (how much, to whom?)
- What resources will I have for a life that offers meaning, purpose and fulfilment?
- Given the choice would I want to retire? If so, at what point?

■ Where do those reflections leave me?

_____

_____

_____

[end activity]

It is now commonplace for individuals or couples in the second half of their lives to say they are 'SKI-ING' (Spending the Kids' Inheritance). Having spent many years and much resource bringing up their offspring and getting them established, the parents are now making sure they are not piling up yet further amounts to bequeath when they go. The airline Lufthansa captured this philosophy brilliantly when they said, in one of their ads:

> *'Fly first-class with Lufthansa! If you don't, your children will.'*

Tips on retiring

An excellent little book *101 Secrets of a Great Retirement* by Mary Helen and Shuford Smith, (McGraw-Hill, New York, 2000) offers wisdom drawn from many retirees whose experience they studied. They say:

> *'If there is nothing else you would rather be doing, then continuing to work will serve you well.'*

So, continuing to do some work is one option, but if we choose not to, or have no choice at all, then we need to embark on retirement with positive attitudes and good planning. One of the retirees in the book just mentioned observed:

> *'Retirement may be one of the greatest changes in our lives and offer us one of the greatest challenges. Yet for most of us, we've only considered how much money we have saved and what trip we would like to take.'*

With good preparation the experience of retirement can be one of moving on to a phase of life which can offer rich opportunities to design a life of great variety and reward. It is a cliché for retired people who get it right to report 'I don't know how I found time for paid work!', but very many do say that. So how to get it right?

See the whole picture

We need to plan beyond just 'playing more golf' or 'having more holidays' and address our retirement years holistically. Some have found a retirement mind map can provide a useful framework for planning. A

mind map is a very useful technique invented by Tony Buzan[10], for working with lots of information and making it manageable. As a way of generating and recording data and making it usable, it beats making lots of lists. Lists are linear and difficult to interconnect, but a mind map is more in tune with the way our brains work i.e. not in straight lines but spontaneous, multi-dimensional and interconnecting.

Here is a mind map compiled by someone planning ahead for retirement and facing a whole range of key questions.

10 See www.imindmap.com

Retirement Mind Map

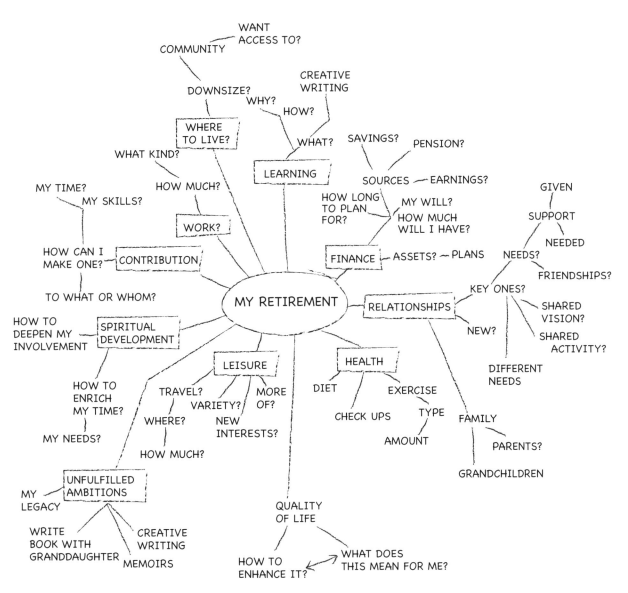

You can see that the mind map method:

- Can contain masses of diverse but interconnected ideas with the main themes clearly defined
- Can ease the task of selecting priorities and areas to work on whilst seeing the 'big picture'
- Offers more coherence whilst being easy to add to or expand.

Activity 1.11

My mind map

If you are contemplating or facing retirement, building your own mind map could alert you to some of the areas you will need to address. Here's how!

- Working on a large sheet of paper put the title of your mind map right at the centre – 'My retirement'.
- To that centre add the heading for the first of the themes you will think through – think in terms of branch lines leaving the main line stations and heading outwards to suburbs. Start anywhere with any topic.
- Write the theme heading in capitals or in a particular colour.
- Reflecting on the relevant areas of your life in retirement, let your mind flow around each theme and develop your line of thought leading outwards. As thoughts come to mind enter the key words on the line.

Think through and build your mind map around the different areas of your life that will comprise and affect your life in retirement. Take your time, it is valuable work! No-one ever gets a mind map 'right' or neat the first time, so we would suggest doing one in rough and in pencil, until you are satisfied you have all of the elements you want to include.

When you have completed your mind map, study it carefully and as you do write in your thoughts on the following:

■ What did I become aware of or what occurred to me as I compiled my retirement mind map?

_____

_____

_____

■ Who will be the key people in my life and what can I do to maintain and enhance those relationships?

_____

_____

_____

■ What standard of living will be available for me in my retirement? What, if anything might I need to find out now? What adjustments if any might I need to make? Who could help me now with financial planning?

_____

_____

_____

■ What are the areas which will give me most life satisfaction? What will be the key areas to which I need to give attention to ensure my best quality of life?

_____

_____

_____

■ What do I need to work on now to make sure I am ready to retire when I want to and if I have to?

_____

_____

_____

[end activity]

Whatever you decide about retirement, here are some tips from people who have made it work for them:

Plan to be as active as you can, in mind and body
Retiring to do 'nothing', which might be a temptation after a long and busy working life, could do more harm than good. Our bodies and our brains need purposeful, satisfying activity. Do not confuse freedom with idleness. Also, avoid trying to cram everything into the first six months and then running out of steam.

Look for balance and variety
Golf every day or too much travel might just lose its attraction. Balance exercise for the body with stimulus for the mind; time away with time at home; social time with personal time; sound with quiet; town with country; rest with exercise; indulgence with moderation; looking after oneself with caring for others; work with play.

Don't change everything at once
Some change can be exciting; too much change can be stressful. It is sometimes tempting in retirement to 'up and off' – the cottage by the sea at the place we've always loved, life in the country, a house abroad. But we may not just be moving house; we can also be leaving behind friends, family, communities we were used to, accessible services. We then have whole new contexts to come to terms with, at just the time when familiar circumstances may be more important than ever before. Psychologists suggest that having a sound 'stability zone' in our lives counts for a great deal and can help us manage change effectively. Sound, established relationships, familiar places, support close at hand can help us adventure at intervals.

Live positively
Be alert to how you think about the world, yourself, other people and challenges that come your way. Seeing problems as challenges, seeing the good in people; seeing the fun in younger people; having a laugh at yourself and situations you face; engage with happy people. At the end of the day do a quick audit; how much did I laugh today; how much did I moan; how much did I mix with people who bring a smile; how much with people who complain ; what did I do today to make others happy? How can I make tomorrow even more positive for myself and somebody else?

Plan ahead
Have a vision of yourself doing positive, exciting things in the future. The inspirational Jane Tomlinson, who was diagnosed with terminal cancer at the age of 27, decided she was not going to die before she had demonstrated to her young children just how much she could achieve and provide for them as a model of how to live. She spent the next 16 years accomplishing amazing athletic achievements and raising vast amounts for good causes. Having our own vision of ourselves achieving positive things (in our terms) in the years ahead, even though we are much older than Jane, gives us a very good chance of living remarkably ourselves.

> _'Over the years, we create a rich milieu that includes walks, hikes, dances, conversations, letters, books, discussion groups and worthwhile projects. We take time to interact with nature. We put love and affection at the top of our lists. We attempt new ventures. We reflect. We show appreciation. We continue to make our dreams real.'_
>
> Mary Helen and Shuford Smith
> _'101 Secrets for a Great Retirement'_

my finances
my relationships
my learning
my health and wellbeing
my leisure
my spirituality

Keep learning

The world moves fast and we should challenge ourselves to keep up with it. Using our brains and our bodies is the best way of keeping them functioning? There are now so many wonderful learning opportunities available. Many now do degrees in their 60s, 70s and 80s and love the stimulation of learning alongside young undergraduates. The World Wide Web is a fantastic resource that we can have in our homes, an amazing source of information on so many topics. Local adult education courses and lifelong learning opportunities offer a vast variety of scope for us to learn new skills and new knowledge at a stage in our lives when we are likely to have the time and resource we never had previously.

Portfolio living

Portfolio living is recognised as the lifestyle of the future. If we grew up in a generation which thought in terms of a job-for-life and then retirement, then we may find the concept both challenging and fascinating. Many of us come from an era when many people, and most definitely our parents:

- Spent most of their working life in one career sector (e.g. financial services, retail, manufacturing, engineering, teaching etc)

- Went, most days, to a place of work from 9 to 5 and worked a five-day week

- Climbed a promotion ladder which rewarded length of service and loyalty to an organisation which offered security

- Had company pension schemes related to final salary

- Retired at 65, hopefully to a life of leisure.

That culture offered us predictability and did little to prepare us for a world in which:

- Certainty has disappeared and been replaced by variety and flexibility

- Security is no longer guaranteed in any walk of life and we are required to be largely self-sufficient; the reverse side of that security coin was dependence

- Permanence has been replaced by rapid change in all aspects of life

- Little choice has become massive choice and people want and expect more out of life

- Retirement at 65 is more of a rarity; some get there earlier, some later.

That sudden cut-off of a working life at 65 and its replacement by reduced income and a period of minimal activity was, research suggests, probably a recipe for a shortened life. Original pension schemes were actually based on the assumption that the recipients would not live too long after retirement and current reduced levels of annuities on offer recognise that the funds now have to provide for significantly extended life spans.

So, the task for those of us living in the second half of our lives now is to reinvent retirement. We may not have lived 'portfolio lives' so far – but we can certainly design ourselves a 'portfolio retirement' aimed at enriching our bonus years. What are the benefits of portfolio living? Those enjoying such a lifestyle report its virtues as being:

- It is tailored to our unique self, built around our preferences, suiting the pace at which we want to live

- We are 'in charge'; no bosses, no three-line whips, plenty of choice and, if we are lucky, most of what we do is 'chosen'

- Variety; no two days need be the same, unless we want them to be

- It can 'play to our strengths' ; we can focus on what we do well, what we most enjoy

- It can offer a combination of sources from which we can draw purpose and meaning

- Flexibility; we can expand rewarding areas and reduce less attractive ones with ease

- There need not be the 'sudden stop' end to working life and the dive into the deep end of inactive retirement, with all the problems that might bring.

The previous model of retirement instantly replaced a life of full-time paid work with a life of full-time leisure. What we are seeking now is portfolio retirement which will blur that sharp edge, which for some turned out to be a precipice.

OLD MODEL OF RETIREMENT		NEW MODEL OF RETIREMENT
Full-time paid work	*Tapering off*	*Some paid work*
Full stop at 65		Gradual transition
Little unpaid work		More unpaid work
Little leisure		More leisure
Little learning		More learning
Little choice		Plenty of choice
Rigid model		Flexible model

Charles Handy, in his article 'Age of Enlightenment' (*The Guardian* 06/05/06), asserts that the challenge of an ageing population and less-certain pensions will not occur imminently. He says the retirees of the next decade or so, benefiting from a parental generation who became rich on house value inflation:

'will not be poor. They can expect to enter their Third Age of "living", after the first two of learning and working, in good shape. For them the next 10 to 20 years truly will be ones of opportunity. That still leaves them with the question "What will we do?" It is their successor generation who will have to face the added question "What will we live on?"'

Activity 1.12

My retirement portfolio

Work through the following checklist, which lists elements of portfolio living that some of the respondents to our questionnaire have included in their own retirement portfolio. Some may strike you as 'off the wall' – but if you can't be a bit off the wall when you retire, then when can you? Remember: all these are genuine options or ideas.

Ask yourself:

- Which of these options might interest me? Add a tick
- Which will I find out more about? Add a tick
- Could I add to the list things which I have observed that friends or acquaintances have taken up in retirement?

Portfolio retirement checklist	Could interest me	Will explore
Paid work elements		
part-time freelance consultancy to replace full-time with present company		
part-time freelance consultancy with former supplier		
freelance consultancy offering expertise to local businesses		
part-time teaching using expertise in local schools/colleges		
part-time work doing something completely different		
turning an unpaid work skill (e.g. DIY plumbing) into paid freelance		
driving a taxi		
becoming a guide for a company offering specialist tours		
teaching in prisons		
becoming a performance poet		
grape picking in French vineyards		
crewing on a voyage to the Caribbean		

my finances

my relationships

my learning

my health and wellbeing

my leisure

my spirituality

my work options

my finances

my relationships

my learning

my health and wellbeing

my leisure

my spirituality

Portfolio retirement checklist	Could interest me	Will explore
Paid work elements		
leading groups on international fauna and flora trips		
consulting on soil science to former Soviet farms		
fostering or adopting children		
Unpaid work		
range of voluntary work via local Volunteer Bureau		
involvement in local/national politics		
involvement in neighbourhood development/residents association/local campaigns		
exploring and writing family history		
offering time and skills to local or national charities		
organising local art/music/drama/literary events		
coaching local sports teams		
stock market investments		
becoming a spiritual guide		
mentoring in local businesses		
mentoring for the Prince's Trust		
starting a housing association to address local needs		
teaching reading to support teachers in primary schools		
Leisure		
taking up a new sport		
travelling to new parts of the world		
backpacking world tour for a year		
trekking in the Himalayas		
learning a musical instrument		
going on cookery courses		
teaching grandchildren a skill		
performing in local amateur dramatics /musicals		

Portfolio retirement checklist	Could interest me	Will explore
Leisure		
training to be a dry stone wall builder		
taking a degree		
taking GCSE and 'A' levels		
learning digital photography		
qualifying in Masters Ticket (sailing)		
learning watercolour painting		
learning new technology		
creative writing		
film studies		

■ Reflecting on work you have done earlier to identify your skills, interest and values, if you had to compile a portfolio for your ideal retirement, what would you include in it? What would be your ideal combination?

_____

_____

_____

_____

_____

■ Look again at what you have noted and ask yourself whether that combination would give you feelings of achievement, pleasure, satisfaction, fulfilment – what changes might you make to get more of those feelings?

_____

_____

_____

_____

_____

■ What steps would you need to take to make that ambition achievable?

_____

_____

_____

_____

_____

[end activity]

my work options

my finances

my relationships

my learning

my health and wellbeing

my leisure

my spirituality

If we get it right, our retirement can indeed be the 'golden age' at the end of our rainbow!

Finding out more

To find out more about work options including retirement…

See www.encore.org; this website expands the ideas in Marc Freedman's excellent book *Encore – finding work that matters in the second half of your life*.[11] Particularly interesting is their idea of community meetings in which people come together informally to support each other in finding new and meaningful work.

Ask a career and life-planning specialist. Contact a specialist advisor at learndirect by emailing advice-resources@ufi.co.uk or by phoning 0800 100 900.

The Age Employment Network (TAEN) is a major provider of information and is active on behalf of the over 50s www.taen.org.uk.

The Government's Age Positive initiative is also an advocate for our age groups www.agepositive.gov.uk. For help in starting your own business try the Prime Business Club, www.primebusinessclub.co.uk.

Summary

In this section you have:

- Identified your life values
- Checked your life values against your present paid work, unpaid work and other paid or unpaid work possibilities and patterns of employment
- Checked your transferable skills and work interests against the jobs in the 'World of Work map'
- Identified your unpaid work skills
- Checked your skills and interests against unpaid work options
- Looked at the range of employment patterns that exist and decided which is or are the right ones for you
- Examined attitudes towards retirement, identified needs we might have and options for meeting those
- Examined some myths about older workers.

Web resources

- if you have practical skills and are looking for employment or looking for people to do work for you try:
www.the50plus.co.uk
www.fiftyon.co.uk
www.laterlife.com/laterlife-career-management.htm
www.agepositive.gov.uk/jobseeking
www.encorerecruitment.com

- you can also look at:
www.jobsite.co.uk
www.jobcentreplus.gov.uk and
www.2young2retire.com
(this is American but still worth looking at for ideas)

- For retirement issues look at:
www.retirement-matters.co.uk

- www.wiseowls.co.uk takes up the causes of the over 50s and employment and retirement

- for opportunities for part-time volunteering see www.reach-online.org.uk they have over 4,000 opportunities available for volunteers.

- For more information please visit www.fiftyforward.co.uk

11 PublicAffairs Books, June 2007

Action plans

Review the information in the Work section of this programme by looking at your comments noted in the Activities or in your Aha pages at the end of the book.

After thinking about what is there, fill in the following table by writing in what you want more of, less of and what you would like to keep the same in your life right now.

		MORE OF…	LESS OF…	KEEP THE SAME
Paid work	people			
	activities			
Unpaid work	people			
	activities			
My life in general	people			
	activities			
My retirement	people			
	activities			

Pick the three that you would like to start working on right away:

1. _____

2. _____

3. _____

> 'In my 20s and 30s I never had enough time to enjoy the journey – to smell the flowers on the way! In my 40s I was starting to believe in myself and live a more relaxed lifestyle, have more fun. In my 50s I was becoming more of a maverick, doing what I/we chose to do – living my values more comfortably. In my 60s I'm starting to be a bigger 'hooligan' – caring less what people think – life is too short!'
>
> *Jim, in his 60s*

my finances

my relationships

my learning

my health and wellbeing

my leisure

my spirituality

Notes

my finances

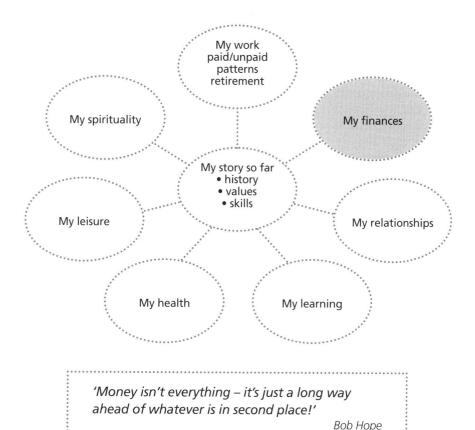

> 'Money isn't everything – it's just a long way ahead of whatever is in second place!'
>
> Bob Hope

Introduction

The over 50s are perhaps the luckiest generation who have ever lived – the longest living, the healthiest, the ones who had the best of the Welfare State, the health and education services, the best of pension arrangements, and the best of the housing boom benefits. All that, and of course we are the wealthiest group in the population with all the benefits that can bring!

That, of course, is the big, generational picture. At the individual level we will have our differences. There will not be too many of us for whom 'money is no object', who are so wealthy that we do not have to think and plan for the rest of our lives. For most of us, there are some key questions to reflect upon:

- How long are we going to live – and for how long can we go on earning?

- Can we fund the lifestyle we would like in the second half of our lives?

- How can we finance the plans or ambitions we are making?

- What provision have we made or should we make for life beyond employment?

- What will our pension be worth?

- Will there be a time when we can neither get, nor do, paid work, when we might need care? Where will that come from, what might it cost?

- What material provision might we want to make – or should we make – for the care of our ageing parents; how much should we help our adult children; should we make any provision for our grandchildren's education?

- How do we make the best use of our assets (our

my work options

my finances

my relationships

my learning

my health and wellbeing

my leisure

my spirituality

property, our savings, our pensions) in the second half of our lives?

- Should we have a will? What do we want to say in it?
- What provision have we made or should we make for partners (or former partners)?
- Will there be 'a rainy day' that we have 'put something by for'?
- How much financial security do we want? How much have we got? Do we need more? How do we get it?

These are not questions we necessarily ponder each day in the first half of our lives. However, they are certainly questions most of us will come face to face with at stages in the second half.

As we plan for the second half of our lives it will be vitally important to ensure that we have the financial base to enable us to do most, if not all, that we want to do.

Were you aware that if a husband is aged 65 and his wife 60 then on average one of them can expect to live to 90? What age are you? What, on average, is likely to be your life span? Are you financially prepared for such longevity?

As with dieting, where most of us actually have little idea what we actually eat, many of us only have a rough estimate of what we spend. The first activity in this theme will provide a simple spreadsheet to enable you to get an accurate picture of your current financial situation.

Knowing what income we have, and what we spend, is only the first step. Activity 2.1 asks you to begin to assess just what returns you are getting from the ways you spend your money and your time. If you want more out of life than you are currently getting, then one of your options may be to cut down on the time you are doing paid work. This probably means, however, that you will have to cut down on your expenditure. This activity should enable you to make decisions as to how to simplify your life and live with less income if you so choose.

Do you know?

- A recent survey of 12 developed and 12 developing countries showed that 41% of people in their 40s and 50s, and 33% of those in their 60s and 70s, have provided financial support to a relative or friend over the previous six months.

- Among those providing financial support, 42% of those in their 40s and 50s (and 44% of those in their 60s and 70s) provide financial support to children; 16% of those in their 60s (and around 30% of those in their 70s) provide financial support to grandchildren. One-third of those in their 40s and 50s provide support to other family members, mainly parents.

- Nearly half of those in their 60s and 70s provide financial support to other family members, mainly children. So much for the idea that our children have to support us!

- The pensioners' income survey in 2007 shows that retired people are wealthier than ever. Over the past 26 years, the real income of retired people has risen every year by between 2.5% and 3%. Newly retired people are much better off than those now aged 75+.

- Pensioners' income comes from five sources:
  - state pension 45%
  - occupational or personal pension 28%
  - 16% comes from paid work which many pensioners still do
  - investment income 9%
  - other sources 2%.

- A 1977 report into pensioners' savings revealed that the average pensioner had £878.68 in personal savings. The equivalent in 2005 showed that this figure had risen to £12,911.10.

- According to ONS Focus on Old People: 'The average net income of pensioners grew faster than that for non-pensioners between 1979 and 2002/03. In 1979, 47% of pensioners were in the bottom fifth of the net income distribution. By 2002/03, this proportion had almost halved to 26%.

- Over the last eight years, pensioners' incomes in Great Britain have risen faster than average earnings. Net pensioner income rose by 28% between 1995/96 and 2003/04. The increase was even sharper after deducting housing costs, rising by 38% over the period. The growth in pensioner incomes over the period resulted from substantial increases in income from occupational pensions and benefits.

- The levels of income older people receive falls with age. The median net household income for people aged 50–59 was £353 a week in 2003/04, compared with £232 for people over 80 (after

my work options

my finances

my relationships

my learning

my health and wellbeing

my leisure

my spirituality

housing costs and adjusted for household size).

- The proportion of pensioners living on low incomes in Great Britain has fallen over the past decade, from 26% in 1995/96 to 20% in 2003/04.

- People in their 50s get most of their income from employment and self-employment (80%). This falls to just 10% for those in their 70s. State benefits (which include the state retirement pension) are the main source of income for pensioners. The majority of pensioners have additionally some form of private income.

- Pensioner couples, on average, have over twice as much investment and private pension income as single pensioners. Younger pensioners tend to have higher incomes than older pensioners, because they are more likely to receive private pension and earnings income than older pensioners, and at a higher level.

- Between 1965 and 2006 there have been some notable changes in the way that both 50–64s and over 65s spend their money and their time. Their spending patterns have diversified and are no longer concerned with just the basics of life. Notably, the over 50s' propensity to spend has vastly increased; they now spend over double the amount that they did in the 1950s. Again, this emphasises the growing importance of this group, not only in demographic terms, but also as high-spending consumers.

- In 1965, food made up just over 20% of the total expenditure of the 50–64 age group; in 2006 food represented just under 12%. We can see a similar trend in expenditure on housing, fuel, light and power, with particularly the over 65s decreasing their percentage spend on these items.

- Where we are seeing increases in spending is on durable household goods (such as TVs) and transport and services. This suggests that less is being spent on the basics and instead, these age groups are splashing out on items such as new TVs or SkyPlus boxes. People over 50 now spend almost £3,000 per year, on average, on these items.

- Of further interest is that one of the biggest areas of both 50–64 and over 65s' spending is on 'services': it makes up 10% and 12% of spending respectively. This is almost double the percentage of spending in 1965. If we calculate the average spend on these per week, this comes to £70.30 for 50–64s and £80 for 65+. This means that these

two age groups spend £3,655.60 and £4,160 respectively on 'luxury' products per year, which include package holidays and hairdressing.

- The predominant alcoholic drink bought has also changed over the last 50 years, with beer/cider making up 63% of spending on alcohol in 1965 compared with just 20% in 2006. It is now wine/spirits which are the most popular for those over 50, with 80% of alcohol spend going on this – a total average cost of £30 a month.

- Over half of the over 50s own their homes outright; just under a quarter were buying their home with a mortgage.

- US research recently is suggesting that we are all being encouraged to save too much and that we need nothing like the amounts that government, and in particular the financial institutions, are demanding that we save.

Laurence Kotlikoff, an economics professor at Boston University, says that standard retirement calculators 'wildly' overestimate how much people need to save for retirement. 'They can easily tell a middle-class couple to save four times more than they should,' said Kotlikoff, who has spent more than a decade developing his own retirement savings estimator that he's now trying to market. He says the industry embraces 'unbelievably crude' methods for setting savings goals – partly out of ignorance, but also out of greed, using scare tactics to pump up sales of mutual funds.

John Karl Scholz, economics professor at the University of Wisconsin at Madison, contends that most Americans are preparing well for retirement.

'There's no huge retirement savings crisis,' Scholz said. 'Most people are roughly getting it right.' 'Even a casual reading of the financial press would give one the perception that households weren't preparing well for retirement,' he said. The crux of the problem, according to Scholz, is the industry rule of thumb that maintains retirees will need annual income equal to 75% to 85% of their pre-retirement income. This so-called replacement rate calculation assumes 'all the spending the person does before retirement will continue all the years after retirement, including money spent raising children, paying for college and paying down a mortgage'.

Using a test case, Kotlikoff's analysis showed Fidelity's online calculator set savings targets 36% higher than his calculator. Vanguard, the insurance company,

my work options

my finances

my relationships

my learning

my health and wellbeing

my leisure

my spirituality

overestimated by 53%, he said, while TIAA-CREF and American Funds – another mutual fund giant – set targets that were 78% too high. Does the same apply to the UK?

According to recent research by Government website Directgov, over half of UK adults have no idea how much money they've built up in pension schemes – and one in six people have no details of where their money is saved. The national survey found that one of the main reasons for losing track of pensions is the number of times people change jobs and also that they believe if a pension exists, it is not worth much.

However, people can be pleasantly surprised if they decide to trace previous pensions. Tony Douglas, a 59-year-old civil servant from Newcastle, thought his old pension scheme was worthless until he used the pension tracing service via Directgov and discovered it was worth £25,000.

Commenting on the research, Nicolas Owen, BBC News Presenter said: 'Your pension is one of the most important financial assets you have, so it's simply astonishing to hear that so many people are losing track of their money throughout their professional lives. Excuses given range from being disorganised, to moving house, to thinking they are worthless, but the fact is that this is your future – your retirement, so it is vital that you track these funds down. It is estimated that there is a large pot of money out there, so it's worth going on Directgov to see if you have a share of this sum.'

To put work and income into perspective, it is interesting to read the work of Marshall Sahlins, author of *Stone Age Economics*, 1972. He discovered that, historically, men appeared to hunt for two and a half days a week with an average work week of 15 hours. Women gathered for about the same time. In fact, one day's work supplied a woman's family with vegetables for the next three days. Throughout the year, both men and women worked for a couple of days, then took a couple of days off to rest and play games, gossip, engage in rituals and visit one another. The industrial revolution changed all of that!

Something to think about...

In a recent one-hour interview on CNBC with Warren Buffet, the second richest man in the world – and who has donated $31 billion to charity – we learned some interesting aspects of his life.

- He bought his first share at age 11 – and he now regrets that he started too late!

- He bought a small farm at age 14, with savings from delivering newspapers

- He still lives in the same small three-bedroom house in mid-town Omaha that he bought after he got married 50 years ago. He says that he has everything he needs in that house. His house does not have a wall or a fence

- He drives his own car everywhere and does not have a driver or security people around him.

- He never travels by private jet, although he owns the world's largest private jet company.

- His company, Berkshire Hathaway, owns 63 companies. He writes only one letter each year to the CEOs of these companies, giving them goals for the year.

- He never holds meetings or calls them on a regular basis. He has given his CEOs only two rules:

  Rule number 1: do not lose any of your shareholders' money.

  Rule number 2: do not forget rule number 1.

- Buffet does not socialise with the high society crowd. His pastime after he gets home is to make himself some popcorn and watch television.

- Bill Gates, the world's richest man, met him for the first time only five years ago. Bill Gates did not think he had anything in common with Warren Buffet, so he had scheduled his meeting for only half an hour. When Gates met him, the meeting lasted for ten hours and Bill Gates became a devotee of Warren Buffet.

- Warren Buffet does not carry a mobile phone, nor has he a computer on his desk.

His advice to young people:

'Stay away from credit cards and invest in yourself and remember:

A. Money doesn't create man but it is man who created money.

B. Live your life as simple as you are.

C. Don't do what others say, just listen to them; do what you feel is good.

D. Don't go on brand name; just wear those things in which you feel comfortable.

E. Don't waste your money on unnecessary things, rather just spend on those who are really in need.'

my work options

my finances

my relationships

my learning

my health and wellbeing

my leisure

my spirituality

Activity 2.1

What do I earn, what do I spend and what do I need?

A major barrier to us getting what we want out of life is the belief that we cannot afford to live on less than we currently earn or receive.

This activity will help you to record specific data on your outgoings and your income and then, crucially, invites you to assess just what you get from each of these expenditures.

We have included a spreadsheet for you to use. You can use the one below but you may be better off creating your own, so that you can write in your own categories. If you have a computer with a spreadsheet this would be the ideal way of doing it. Any spreadsheet program will do. If you have internet access then a spreadsheet is online at **www.fiftyforward.co.uk** so that you can input your own data or change the categories etc. This spreadsheet will do all of the adding up for you and will also show you, for example, just what percentage of income you spend in total that you spend on alcohol, or utilities or holidays! You can change any of the headings that we have used so that they better reflect the language that fits for you. You can also insert or delete lines by right-clicking any of the lines and choosing *insert* or *delete*.

Note: the next piece of work involves considerable preparation to be able to complete it accurately.

We suggest that you budget for a year. Look at your bills for last year, your direct debits, your cheque books and bank statements. Look at gas, electricity, water charges. Look at your council tax charges, your rent/mortgage outgoings, etc. Work out the totals for the year and place a 12th in each month. Estimate for the other items – money spent on holidays, on eating out, on entertainment, on travel, on insurance, on the costs of running your car(s) etc, and insert the average monthly spend. Most of us underestimate how much we spend on food and drink – and also on clothes and going out. See what you find.

YEAR 20 _ _	JAN	FEB	MAR	APR	MAY	JUN	JUL	AUG	SEP	OCT	NOV	DEC	TOTAL	% of total
WHAT YOU SPEND														
HOUSEHOLD														
rent/mortgage														%
food & entertaining														%
take away meals														%
alcohol/tobacco, etc														%
house insurance														%
contents insurance														%
water rates														%
dry cleaning/cleaning														%
house repairs														%
new house items														%
telephones														%
gas														%
electricity														%
council tax														%
DIY materials														%
pets														%
TOTAL														%
ENTERTAINMENT														
books/mags/subs														%
cd/dvd/games														%
TV licence/ rental														%
gardening items														%
meals out														%
theatre/cinema/events														%
holidays														%

my work options
my finances
my relationships
my learning
my health and wellbeing
my leisure
my spirituality

YEAR 20 _ _	JAN	FEB	MAR	APR	MAY	JUN	JUL	AUG	SEP	OCT	NOV	DEC	TOTAL	% of total
WHAT YOU SPEND														
ENTERTAINMENT														
sports														%
learning														%
travel insurance														%
TOTAL														%
FAMILY														
child 1														%
child 2														%
child 3														%
parents														%
other family														%
friends														%
presents														%
TOTAL														%
CAR/TRAVEL														
car tax														%
fuel														%
vehicle insurance														%
breakdown insurance														%
repayments														%
repairs														%
buses														%
trains														%
taxis														%
TOTAL														%

YEAR 20 _ _	JAN	FEB	MAR	APR	MAY	JUN	JUL	AUG	SEP	OCT	NOV	DEC	TOTAL	% of total
WHAT YOU SPEND														
HEALTH & HYGIENE														
prescriptions														%
health/sports club, etc														%
health insurance														%
hairdressing, etc														%
TOTAL														%
MONEY MATTERS														
pensions														%
lottery/gambling														%
charity														%
stationery/postage														%
savings														%
TOTAL														%
CLOTHES														
clothes														%
shoes														%
dry cleaning/laundry														%
TOTAL														%
MISCELLANEOUS														%
GRAND TOTAL														%

YEAR 20 _ _	JAN	FEB	MAR	APR	MAY	JUN	JUL	AUG	SEP	OCT	NOV	DEC	TOTAL
WHAT YOU EARN													
state pension													
occupational pension													
state benefits													
paid work													
bank interest													
dividends													
premium bonds/lotteries, etc													
expenses													
building society interest													
gifts													
grants or loans, other sources													
GRAND TOTAL													
BALANCE													

my work options

my finances

my relationships

my learning

my health and wellbeing

my leisure

my spirituality

■ What does the picture tell you about your financial situation?

_____

_____

_____

_____

_____

_____

■ What would you like to change?

_____

_____

_____

_____

_____

_____

■ What might you need to change?

_____

_____

_____

_____

_____

_____

■ What will it take to make the changes you want or need?

_____

_____

_____

_____

_____

_____

[end activity]

Activity 2.2

What am I getting out of life for my money?

It's now time to see just what you are getting for the money you are spending. At the far right of your spreadsheet add three columns. Head them:

- **Essential**
- **Nice to have**
- **Can I spend less?**

If you are using the website (**www.fiftyforward.co.uk**), click on 'financial health check' again and you will see that at the right-hand side of the table are the three columns. The headings are already there for you.

Go to the first new column (Essential) and write/type in an X by each one you believe to be essential to the way you want to live your life.

The next column asks you which of these items are 'nice to have'. Again write/type in an X as appropriate.

The third column is asking you if you could spend less on that item. You can choose between giving it a 1, which means 'absolutely not', 2, which means 'to some extent', 3, which means 'significantly' and 4, which means that you could 'totally' reduce or even eliminate that item.

■ What do you realise as a result of this activity?

_____

_____

_____

_____

■ Are you surprised by anything that you have found from this activity?

_____

_____

_____

_____

_____

■ Which are the items that you could cut down on or get rid of if you chose to do so?

_____

_____

_____

_____

_____

[end activity]

my work options

my finances

my relationships

my learning

my health and wellbeing

my leisure

my spirituality

my finances (iv) work options

my relationships

my learning

my health and wellbeing

my leisure

my spirituality

The challenge for you will then be to convert some of these thoughts into *objectives* – and to develop action plans to achieve them. (See the 'Bringing it all together' chapter on page 181.)

Many of us trap ourselves into a lifestyle because of assumptions we make of what we must have before life is worthwhile. Our 'hunger' can sometimes be so consuming that we pursue goals which are not in our best interests and not even in line with our life values.

How do I cut down on my spending?

The previous activity should have helped you to identify some ways that you might cut down on your spending – if you wish to do so. We are certainly not advocating that everyone should cut down on their spending. It only becomes important if the way you are currently investing your time and energies is not giving you what you want.

www.fiftyforward.co.uk, by linking up with www.horsesmouth.co.uk, provides opportunities of talking to other people on how we can make do with less if that then gives us the freedom to make some other life and work choices. Look at the website section on mentoring which will take you there.

Tips to save money

- Explore what you want to buy in stores and then buy it on the internet at home. Use your search engines.

- Always negotiate in smaller stores. You can try in the larger stores, but the sales people often have no delegated power to negotiate with you.

- Ask for discounts for cash.

- Try home exchange schemes instead of renting villas and houses.

- Forget designer labels and go to TK Maxx, Primark, George at Asda, etc.

- Don't buy new. You can buy secondhand copies of books from Amazon online that are hugely discounted from the price of new ones.

- Pay off your credit cards. The interest rates are horrendous.

- Use public transport instead of your car.

- Try using a carpool to get to work. Set one up.

- Always shop around for insurance cover, utilities, and telephone service providers. Use www.uswitch.com or www.energyhelpline.com on the internet.

- Sign up for Martin Lewis' Money Saving Tips www.moneysavingexpert.com. He also has a couple of excellent books on saving money. Buy them secondhand on Amazon – or borrow them from a library.

- Don't change your car every two to three years. Keep it on the road for ten years and run it into the ground.

- Swap services with people you know, e.g. hair-dressing for babysitting, cleaning for bookkeeping, etc.

- Sign up for www.petrolprices.com for the latest pump prices at service stations close to your postcode.

- Use email instead of letters.

Finding out more

Ask around for a recommendation for a specialist financial advisor.

Although American, it is well worth reading *Your Money or Your Life*, by Joe Dominguez and Vicki Robin – available on Amazon from one penny upwards if bought secondhand – but there will be delivery charges!

> ### Web resources
>
> - For help in reducing energy bills try www.uswitch.com and www.energyhelpline.com
>
> - For help with pension queries try www.pensioncalculator.org.uk
>
> - For annuity queries go to www.fsa.gov.uk
>
> - For retirement issues go to www.retirement-matters.co.uk or www.direct.gov.uk/en/Over50s/RetirementAnd Pensions/PlanningForRetirement/index.htm
>
> - For more information please visit www.fiftyforward.co.uk

Summary

In this section you will have worked out:

- How much you earn and how much you spend

- What your total assets are

- What you are getting out of your life from the money you spend.

Action plans

Review the information in this theme.

After thinking about what is there fill in the following table by writing in what you want more of, less of and what you would like to keep the same in your life right now.

	MORE OF...	LESS OF...	KEEP THE SAME
Things			
Income			

Pick the three that you would like to start working on right away:

1. _____

2. _____

3. _____

my work options

my finances

my relationships

my learning

my health and wellbeing

my leisure

my spirituality

Notes

my relationships

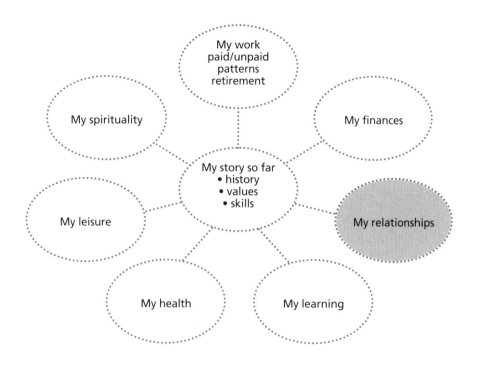

Introduction

Talking to the folks next door could be worth the equivalent of earning an extra £40,000 per year. Maybe you are muttering, 'you don't know my neighbours!' Whatever, in recent research[12], reported by Roger Dobson in *The Times*, June 2007, economists got people to put a value on the relationships and other factors in their life and then linked this to how they much they might value salary increases other than in money terms. Put another way, participants were asked what monetary amount they would regard as being of equivalent value to particular features of their lives.

Based on this theoretical trade-off, their answers suggested that we would value the following.

- **Good health** as being worth the equivalent of £251,000 a year.

- **Excellent health** as being worth the equivalent of £304,000 a year.

12 Article based on 'Putting a price Tag on Friends, Relatives and Neighbours.' Dr Nattavudh Powdthavee, April 2007, *Journal of Social Economics*.

- **Marriage** as being worth the equivalent of £53,833 a year.

- **Living together** as being worth the equivalent of £82,500 a year (more highly valued than marriage!).

- **Separation** as being worth *minus* the equivalent of £57,667 a year (the separated had the lowest levels of life satisfaction).

- **Divorce** as being worth *minus* the equivalent of £24,500 a year.

- Being **widowed** as being *minus* the equivalent of £200,000 a year (the loss of a spouse has one of the biggest effects on health and lifestyle).

- **Meeting friends and relatives**:

  - once or twice a month, worth the equivalent of £35,000 a year

  - once or twice a week, worth the equivalent of £50,500

  - most days, worth the equivalent of £63,833 a year.

my work options

my finances

my relationships

my learning

my health and wellbeing

my leisure

my spirituality

Additionally, in the research currently going on into the subject of happiness, the findings are that, after a certain level of economic wellbeing, it isn't money that brings us happiness. The key ingredients, in order, appear to be:

1. Family and friends (having strong, deep and wide relationships, the deeper and wider the better)

2. Meaning in life (having a belief in something 'bigger than ourselves' such as religion, spirituality or a strong philosophy of life)

3. Goals in life (that are aligned with our values, that lead us to do enjoyable, interesting work or be involved in activities using our strengths and skills)[13].

So, while work and career might matter a great deal to us, it is likely to be the *relationships* in our lives that have a great deal to do with our happiness and life satisfaction. Indeed, across the whole of our lives, our mental and physical health, our longevity and our all-round wellbeing, will be greatly linked to the extent and quality of the relationships we have. We focus in other parts of this book on jobs and career choices, but any decisions we make there will not be made in a vacuum. They will impact on, and will most probably need to take into consideration, our closest family, partners and (possibly) friends. Those we interact with need to be part of our thinking and potentially they can be a very major part of our resources. So, we need to be skilled in how we manage our relationships.

> *'Always remember that a person you deal with today may come back in a different capacity later; how you have dealt with the previous transaction will determine your later transaction, i.e. always treat others as you would want to be treated, always with dignity left intact. Protect the self-belief of any individual's we interact with, self-belief is the most important facet of any individual's esteem.'*
>
> *Ian Walker, in his 50s*

There is increasing interest in the concept of 'social capital' and its link with the wellbeing of society, organisations, the work place and individuals and it is worth just expanding on a few terms:

- **Physical capital** is the equipment, the tools and the plant that contribute to production

- **Human capital** is the workforce that makes the production happen

- **Social capital** is the network of individuals, formal and informal groups and organisations, that combine and cooperate to provide the context and support which underpin society, the workplace and the economy.

Where social capital is strong, then trust and cooperation between people is high, people feel more secure, productive and connected and 'housed, healthy, hired and happy'[14].

We can most valuably see our lives as addressing a range of primary life roles and relationships. In career and life planning terms these are recognised in the following way.

- **Child:** we are born into this role and it can continue quite late into our life, as long as our parents are alive. In fact, as our parents age and increasingly need our support we can become extremely conscious of the demands made on us by our child role.

- **Student/learner:** much of our early life and, in the era of lifelong learning, some of our mid and later life also, will be spent in education, on-the-job learning or training and informal learning.

- **Leisure-user:** parts of our life will be spent on chosen activities outside our paid and unpaid work.

- **Citizen:** time we spend making our contribution to community, civic and national matters and requirements.

- **Volunteer:** committing some of our time and our life to contributing our skills and talents to causes or groups we admire or believe in.

- **Paid worker:** obviously a very major role in the lives of most of us; earning our living and making a contribution to the organisations we work in and those they provide for.

- **Retiree:** the time of our life where we leave behind full-time paid work.

- **Partner:** most of us will commit to one or more long-term relationships during our lifetime.

- **Parent:** most of us will have children, or possibly

13 Based on the work of Professor Ed Diener as reported on http://news.bbc.co.uk/player/nol/newsid_4810000/newsid_4812700/481274 2.stm?bw=bb&mp=wm&news=1

14 2006 M Woolcock in *The search for empowerment. Social Capital as idea and practice at the World Bank* (Anthony Bebbington, M Woolcock, S Guggenheim and E. Olson (eds.) West Hartford. Kumarian

adopt children or have stepchildren. Economic and social changes are lengthening the prominence of this role by delaying the independence of offspring and extending their expectation of emotional and financial support into the second half of their parents' lives.

- **Grandparent:** increasingly, grandparents are engaged with their grandchildren and with supporting their adult offspring in their parent role.

- **Friend:** as our communities become more insular and detached, the role of loyal and trusted friends becomes ever more significant. We will need them ourselves and we will have to be them to others.

- **Carer:** for an increasing number of people caring is becoming a major life role.

It is in our capacity to achieve success in these roles, and perhaps even more in our ability to balance, integrate and harmonise them, that we are likely to measure our life-satisfaction and happiness.

'You can kiss your family and friends goodbye and put miles between you, but at the same time you carry them with you in your heart, your mind, your stomach, because you do not just live in a world, but a world lives in you.'

Frederick Buechner

Do you know?

- Most workers are feeling a time squeeze. In 2003, the Work Foundation found that nearly three-quarters of full-time workers want to spend more time with their families.

- A third of full- and part-time workers report feeling so tired when they get home that they fall asleep during the evening.

- 'Time sovereignty' – the ability to control *when* one works – is regarded as important as the number of hours one works.

- The DTI found that 94% of employers agreed that people work best when they can achieve a good work–life balance.

- Best practice in achieving work–life balance results in reduced absenteeism, less staff turnover and a more productive, committed workforce. (All the above data via **www.employersforwork-lifebalance.org.uk**)

- 20% of people take work home almost every day.

33% of partners of people who work more than 48 hours a week feel this has a negative effect on their personal relationships. Only 33% of all workers say their employer has family-friendly practices or personal support services. (CIPD surveys)

- American sociologists have reported what they call 'a dramatic drop' in people's experience of having 'close confidants' (people they can turn to for help, advice or just as a sounding board; those with whom they can discuss matters that are important to them). People now have 30% fewer people they feel they can turn to than was the case 25 years ago.

- People have fewer contacts with neighbours, clubs and organisations outside the home.

- The decline has been mostly in the number of friends and has resulted in people expecting and needing more support from their immediate family. The decline has been put down to people spending more time working and possibly to increased use of the internet for communication, reducing the need for people to actually meet up. (This is somewhat debatable, as for many the ability now to communicate online with family and friends can extend our social networks.)

- Increasing longevity has led to growing numbers of 'long skinny' families, characterised by an increasing number of four- or five-generation families, with fewer people in each generation. (**www.guardian.co.uk/society**)

- These families have more vertical than horizontal linkages, and are sometimes referred to as 'beanpole families'. In addition, beanpole families often join together through remarriage to form reconstituted families.

- While we may have fewer brothers, sisters and cousins, we also have more living parents, grandparents and great-grandparents than ever before; and we now have the opportunity to enjoy an array of new relationships with half-brothers and sisters, step-brothers and sisters, step-parents and children, step-grandparents and grandchildren and step-cousins.

- While some commentators lament the decline and break-up of the family, in many ways it is thriving. Indeed, in the mature economies of North America and Europe, the family is still central.

- Families still live together, still holiday and socialise together, still take responsibility for bearing children

my work options

my finances

my relationships

my learning

my health and wellbeing

my leisure

my spirituality

my work options
my finances
my relationships
my learning
my health and wellbeing
my leisure
my spirituality

and bringing them up – still, in fact, provide almost all children's financial, emotional and practical support.

- Their members still help each other, bequeath property to each other and provide the majority of support and care to older people.

- The percentage of people who talk only to family members about important matters has risen from 57% to nearly 80%.

- In the UK, 90% of people over 65 are grandparents. They often provide day care for their grandchildren when the children's parents are working or studying. A recent study conducted by Age Concern England found that one in four grandparents care for their grandchildren on a regular basis.

- The National Statistics Omnibus Survey reported that 60% of grandparents looked after grandchildren younger than 15.

'In my 60s and 70s it is great to see my children so happy and successful and to know that they 'rate' me. And grandchildren are the most tremendous bonus in one's later years.'

Phillipa, in her 70s

- Only a small proportion of grandparents (2%) have no contact with grandchildren. There are no significant differences between men and women in the frequencies of having contact with grandchildren, though grandfathers were less likely to meet grandchildren when they were not living with their wives. (**www.grandparents-association.org.uk** and **www.proudgrandparents.co.uk**)

- Divorce rates have risen significantly faster among the over 50s than any other age group in the last 20 years. 7% of the over 60s have tried internet dating.

- Research on 7,000 men and women by the Netherlands Institute of Mental Health and Addiction, shows that in the first year of bereavement almost 22% of the widowed had a major depression, 12% had symptoms of post-traumatic stress disorder and the rest had nine times more likelihood of developing an anxiety disorder.

- Social support is shown to be linked to the quality of life and wellbeing. Family support, followed by friends' support, is most closely related to wellbeing for all age groups.

- 14 million Americans are caring for ageing family members whilst being employed full time or part time themselves. It is estimated that up to ten million adult children are caring for their parents from a long distance.

- The average length of time spent on caring is about eight years, with about one-third of carers providing care for ten years or more

- About 44% of Americans between the ages of 45 and 55 have ageing parents or in-laws, as well as children under 21. They are part of the 'sandwich generation' – stuck between conflicting demands of raising children and caring for failing parents. The tension between the roles is particularly stressful. (For an alternative view of the 'sandwich generation' see Mark Trust 'Something to chew on' **www.theMatureMarket.com**).

The effect of parents' social relationships on their children is interesting:

- Children of sociable parents were between one and four per cent ahead of peers whose parents led more solitary lives.

- Children with good social skills perform better at school than those who lack them.

- Cheerful, upbeat parents talk to their children more and are more affirming. Children of parents who belonged to sports clubs scored higher in reading, maths and vocabulary. Those whose parents did voluntary work scored better in maths and reading. Those whose parents were on school committees scored higher in reading and vocabulary. (Report by Rosemary Bennett on research by Professor Sarah Brown and Karl Taylor of the University of Sheffield and Dr Bethan Marshall, *The Times*, March 2008).

'Having someone wonder when you don't come home at night is a very old human need.'

Margaret Mead

Your support networks

The next activity will help you to identify the supportive relationships you have – and where you might need to strengthen your support system. A problem for many of us is that we often expect most of our support to come from one or two people, and this can put a great deal of pressure on those individuals. Also, we need so many different kinds of support that, almost certainly, just a handful of people could not possibly satisfy all of our support needs. We should therefore try to ensure we have a wide support network with a range of competencies and experience.

Activity 3:1

What support do I have?

Look at the different kinds of support that people have suggested they value. Enter the names of people you know who could, or do, provide that type of support for you.

Support	name	name	name	name
A – Someone I can talk through problems with and confide in.				
B – Someone who knows how to get things done, who is practical and experienced.				
C – Someone to take a break with, have a drink or a meal with, to 'get away from it all'.				
D – Someone I can call on in a crisis.				
E – A chat room group or online friends and acquaintances, e.g. through Facebook, Myspace, etc.				
F – Someone who introduces me to new ideas, new interests, new people.				
G – Someone who challenges me to sit up and take a good look at myself.				

my work options

my finances

my relationships

my learning

my health and wellbeing

my leisure

my spirituality

my work options
my finances
my relationships
my learning
my health and wellbeing
my leisure
my spirituality

Support	name	name	name	name
H – Someone who will give me practical or material support.				
I – Someone who would take up my case with local authorities, national bodies, companies, etc. that I am having problems with.				
J – Someone who can make me feel competent and valued.				
K – Someone I can share good news and good feelings with.				
L – Someone, or some group, I can have a really good laugh with.				
M – Someone who is a specialist in my field.				
N – Someone, or a group, who has expertise in areas I need help with (e.g. technology, finance, the family, the law etc).				

O – Fill in here the kind of support you appreciate that is not mentioned above.

_____

_____

_____

_____

_____

_____

_____

_____

_____

[end activity]

Remember that asking for support is a sign of strength!
Too many of us lack the courage to ask, or see having to ask for help as a weakness.

my work options

my finances

my relationships

my learning

my health and wellbeing

my leisure

my spirituality

Activity 3.2

Support in my different life roles

Now look more specifically at the support you have and that you might need in the different life roles that you fill.

Start by choosing one of the following areas of your life to reflect on: *Home, Paid Work, Community*.

■ Think through the life roles that are involved in that area of your life – and the challenges and pressures each role brings.

■ Reflect on the level of challenge in that role that is evident for you at present; score each in the following way:

      1 – if the challenge is present but not significant

      2 – if the challenge is present and is somewhat significant

      3 – if the challenge is present and very significant.

■ Think about the kind of support that would be valuable to you (consult the list of types of support others have experienced as valuable in Activity 3.1).

■ If you receive the kind of support you appreciate, write in the name of the provider in column 4.

■ If you don't have a provider for the type of support you would like, identify possible sources in column 5.

■ In the final column, note what you might need to do to achieve that kind of support.

When you have completed this for *one* area of your life, revisit this and complete the other areas.

My paid work

Roles	Challenge and pressure level 1 to 3	Type of support needed A–O	Current source if any (enter name)	Other potential sources (enter name)	Action plan – what do you need to do?
Worker					

My family roles

Roles	Challenge and pressure level 1 to 3	Type of support needed A–O	Current source if any *(enter name)*	Other potential sources *(enter name)*	Action plan – what do you need to do?
Child					
Partner					
Parent					
Grandparent					
Carer					

My community roles

Roles	Challenge and pressure level 1 to 3	Type of support needed A–O	Current source if any *(enter name)*	Other potential sources *(enter name)*	Action plan – what do you need to do?
Citizen					
Leisure user					
Learner					
Friend					
Volunteer					

(continued)

my work options

my finances

my relationships

my learning

my health and wellbeing

my leisure

my spirituality

Roles	Challenge and pressure level 1 to 3	Type of support needed A–O	Current source if any *(enter name)*	Other potential sources *(enter name)*	Action plan – what do you need to do?
Retiree					

[end activity]

A frequent result of reflections like this is that we find that many of our 'eggs' are 'in one basket'. Most commonly, a partner has to bear the whole brunt of supporting us. They not only provide for most of our emotional, physical and psychological needs, but they often have to 'pick up the pieces' in the evening if we have had a hard day, or sit and watch us in a couch potato or zombie state. Expecting a partner or one person to provide all our support needs:

- Is likely to be very unfair and even stressful to them

- Means we could be missing out on other expertise

- Is high risk because they may not always be there or find the demands too great.

This may need explaining to a partner, because if they care for us they will want to be everything to us. Caring for them might mean us not expecting them to take on the whole task of providing for all our various support needs. And, of course, vice-versa! Discuss it with those you may need to.

The healthiest and most valuable support systems have breadth and depth. They are multi-faceted, diverse, willing and able.

Relationships

A very significant twentieth-century psychologist and therapist, Carl Rogers, established through his work that:

- During our lifetime, healthy human beings pursue an ambition to become all they are capable of becoming; we are always aspiring to be more than we are, to realise all the potential we have

- We are social beings and are affected by, and interact with, those around us – for better or worse

- Healthy-living results from having a *sense of our own worth* (having positive self-esteem, not believing that we are perfect, but that we are worthwhile and significant) and a *recognition of the worth of others* (a recognition that those we relate to and interact with are also of significance and are worthwhile).

Rogers recognised three features of relationships that produced health and wellbeing for those involved in them:

- **Respect:** we behave towards another person in ways that show them that they are valued, significant and worthwhile

- **Understanding:** showing other people that we can understand 'how they see and feel about things'; that we can see their perspective and point of view; that we can see things their way

- **Genuineness:** when relationships are based on openness, honesty, trustworthiness; without deceit or 'mixed messages'.[16]

Rogers maintained that when people are in a relationship in which those three features are present, then they will grow healthily, will feel good about themselves, will learn and develop successfully and will be capable of solving problems and difficulties they are faced with.

16 A web search for Carl Rogers or Carl Rogers' theories will provide more in-depth information.

Rogers did not 'invent' those features of life. His research found that these were the qualities evident in all healthy, healing relationships. Relationships which respect and recognise another person's uniqueness, dignity and worth are what bring out the best in human beings. These are needs in life that are as important to us as food and drink. If we receive them we grow, if we lack them we are likely to struggle. If we relate in these ways towards other people they will grow healthily from that experience.

Rogers established that the most effective therapists, those whose clients recovered most quickly and most effectively, displayed and demonstrated respect, understanding and genuineness. Later research, not surprisingly, said that those 'people-centred' relationships also marked out the best teachers, the best managers, the best doctors and nurses. People learned better, were more motivated to achieve, got better quicker when they were on the receiving end of quality interactions and relationships.

It is interesting to note that 'behaviours' are at the heart of human interaction and are the 'stuff' of relationships. We cannot read each other's minds (maybe thankfully); we just 'read' the way people behave towards us and vice-versa. We hang on to 'words' because they seem to be massively important, but the evidence is that 'non-verbal' behaviours are even more persuasive. Some estimates suggest that up to 90% of communication between us can be in non-verbal signals: our tone of voice, the expression on our face, the look in our eyes, our 'body language'. We might say 'I really like you', but if we look cross, bored, distracted or preoccupied as we say it we are unlikely to be believed. We are always communicating, whether we realise it or not. The way we dress, the way we sit, stand or walk, the way we look (or don't look) at people, as well as what we say and how we say it, will be 'read' by those around us. What messages are we giving out?

Some people seem to be more successful in building relationships than others. Often, such people seem to be more naturally attractive, more outgoing, easier to be with, 'warmer' and more 'sociable'. These are all words to describe people who behave in particular ways. Their attractiveness may all seem somehow magical, mystical or natural to those of us less adept at attracting others, but in fact they have learned (maybe subconsciously) in their upbringing what it takes to 'get on' with other people.

Activity 3.3

Making relationships work (1)

Here are some statements which other people have made about what makes them like their friends or closest relations.

These people:

- 'show they like me, take an interest in me, don't always go on about their own stuff. Being with them makes me feel good.' ☐

- 'listen to me, they see my point of view.' ☐

- 'are dead reliable, you can always depend on them, they don't let you down!' ☐

- 'choose to spend time with me and make time for me.' ☐

- 'are good fun, we can let our hair down and laugh a lot together.' ☐

- 'are loyal, they don't go off me if I get something wrong, they are forgiving.' ☐

- 'go out of their way, take trouble to please me' ☐

- 'are interested in the things I am interested in, we like similar things.' ☐

- 'don't cause me problems, they care about me.' ☐

- 'are generous, it's never all take and no give!' ☐

my work options

my finances

my relationships

my learning

my health and wellbeing

my leisure

my spirituality

my work options

my finances

my relationships

my learning

my health and wellbeing

my leisure

my spirituality

- 'allow me to be myself when I'm with them, I'm free to be me!' ☐

- 'give me space and time, they are hassle free.' ☐

- 'are people it's easy to be with, I know where I am with them.' ☐

- 'are the kind of people where what you see is what you get. Nothing two-faced, nothing 'behind your back'. ☐

Now think of the best relationships in your life, the people you are closest to. Go back over the list, and tick any of the statements which you feel relate to your view of *your* relationships.

Next, consider the following questions.

- What would you have added about the things those you are closest to do or don't do that makes them attractive to you?

  _____

  _____

  _____

  _____

  _____

- What do you think it is that you do or don't do that makes you attractive to them?

  _____

  _____

  _____

  _____

  _____

Check out your answers at some point if that is appropriate.

[end activity]

You might have mentioned good looks and pots of money, because those can be the initial, flip responses but, beyond those more superficial things, we are attracted to people who make us feel good about ourselves, who make us feel worthwhile; people on whom we can depend, who seem to understand and appreciate our unique 'take' on the world. Unless those deeper 'messages', are present for real in a relationship, then the 'looks and money' may not be enough.

Rogers was making us aware of the following things.

- Quality relationships are built on the way we behave towards each other.

- When we behave in ways that make other people

feel special, that show we can be trusted, that show we can look at things 'through their eyes', then people will find that attractive and helpful.

- When people behave in those ways towards us, we will be attracted to them.

- Quality relationships are built upon a mutual exchange of attraction and trust; they are essential to a healthy, happy life.

There is of course another side of that coin. Just as we can behave in ways that build relationships, that help them thrive and prosper, we can also behave in ways that damage or destroy them. Just as relationships can be at the heart of a happy life, they can also be the cause of some of the greatest hurt and pain we experience.

Activity 3.4

Making relationships work (2)

Reflect on the following questions.

■ Which are the relationships that are most special and important at this stage of my life?

_____

_____

_____

■ What do other people do that conveys to me that they regard me as worthwhile or special?

_____

_____

_____

■ What can I continue to do, or do more often, to make those I care most about feel even more special, appreciated and understood?

_____

_____

_____

■ Which are the relationships that matter to me that I might need to give more attention to?

_____

_____

_____

■ What would I need to do to strengthen or repair those? Do I want to do it?

_____

_____

_____

■ Looking at my next phase of my life and career what changes if any do I want to make to the relationships in my life?

_____

_____

_____

■ What will I do about that?

_____

_____

_____

my work options

my finances

my relationships

my learning

my health and wellbeing

my leisure

my spirituality

my work options
my finances
my relationships
my learning
my health and wellbeing
my leisure
my spirituality

An excellent resource for help with relationship issues is www.relate.org.uk.

> *'Love!*
>
> *What a small word for an idea so immense and powerful.*
>
> *It has altered the flow of history, calmed monsters, kindled works of art, cheered the forlorn, turned tough guys to mush, consoled the enslaved, driven strong women mad, glorified the humble, fuelled national scandals, bankrupted robber barons, and made mincemeat of kings.*
>
> *How can love's spaciousness be explained in the narrow confines of one syllable?*
>
> *Love is an ancient delirium, a desire older than civilisation, with taproots spreading into deep and mysterious days.*
>
> *The heart is a living museum. In each of its galleries, no matter how narrow or dimly lit, preserved forever like wondrous diatoms, are our moments of loving and being loved.'*
>
> From A Natural History of Love *by Diane Ackerman*

[end activity]

Understanding happiness

Is our life about the pursuit of happiness? Is happiness achievable? Is happiness related to pleasure? Can money and possessions make us happy? These are the questions that philosophers have wrestled with over centuries – and that human beings have considered, in one way or another, for even longer.

In recent times psychologists, economists – and even politicians – have worked to have greater understanding of the components of happiness. Their findings suggest the following are typical:

- When asked, most people say they are 'fairly happy'.

- A person's own view of their 'happiness level' generally matches their friends' opinion of their happiness level.

Politicians are becoming interested in what makes people happy because it is emerging that economic prosperity (the political theory that 'it's the economy, stupid' that wins elections) is no longer delivering happiness and satisfaction in the general population.

- A poor economy is likely to make people unhappy; a sound economy is not sufficient to make a population happy[17]. Once we have a home, food and clothes, then increased wealth doesn't seem to translate into greater happiness. In the developed world, increased prosperity has been accompanied by people reporting reduced levels of life satisfaction.

'Standards of living have increased dramatically and happiness has increased not at all, and in some cases has diminished slightly. There is a lot of evidence that being richer... isn't making us happier.'

Professor Daniel Kahneman, University of Princeton

- In 2006, an advisor to the Prime Minister predicted that, within ten years, the Government would be being judged on how happy it makes people.

- Governments are becoming increasingly interested in what makes people healthier and happier because that can shape a range of policies. David Halpern, a senior policy adviser to the Downing Street strategy unit in Tony Blair's time in office, has been working on the science of happiness. He suggests that love is a more significant factor in predicting life expectancy than smoking. If we are 'loved' we will be happier, live longer and be more productive. He says 'The single strongest predictor of whether you will be alive in ten years time is whether you say 'yes' to the question, 'does somebody love you?" (*The Observer*, March 2007, 'Government seeks secret of keeping us all happy', Gaby Hinsliff).

17 See the work of Professor Andrew Oswald and Nattavudh Powdthavee on 'Happiness and Economics'. For a summary of the topic a useful starting point can be http://en.wikipedia.org/wiki/Happiness_economics

Current research is exploring the belief that happier people live longer and healthier lives, and have more rewarding relationships and social lives.

- Professor Diener's[18] work indicates that the happiest people may live up to nine years longer than the unhappiest people (by comparison, heavy smoking can knock six years off our longevity).

- Some things like 'retail therapy' or lottery wins can give us short-term pleasure – but that feeling is short lived and we revert to how happy (or unhappy) we were before.

- Comparing ourselves with people who have more than us can make us unhappy. If we have to compare ourselves with anybody, it should be with those on a par with us – and across a range of measures beyond that of material possessions.

- Friendships and good relationships deliver more happiness than income.

- Marriage (presumably a happy one) can add seven years to male longevity and four years to female.

- At the same time, the loss of a spouse, partner or very close friend can result in several years of reduced happiness and may be even longer lasting.

- The loss of a job can affect us for years, even if we find another one.

- Receiving support from others, and giving support to others, can increase our life satisfaction.

- Diener suggests the first cornerstone of happiness is '*wide and deep relationships*' – people who score high on life satisfaction are likely to have close and supportive family and friends.

- The second is '*having meaning in life*'. This meaning may come from 'a belief in something bigger than ourselves, from religion, spirituality or a philosophy of life'. It may also come from satisfaction with meaningful performance at work, or in learning, or in an important role such as homemaker or grandparent. The message for us is 'Be clear what you love doing and do more of it.'

- The third component of happiness is *having goals that are aligned with our values*, that lead us to do enjoyable, interesting work using our strengths and skills, leading us to have a personal satisfaction with ourselves, with our performance, our learning, our growth.

- Some of the level of happiness we can attain will be down to our *genes* (some researchers estimate as much as 40–50% of our capacity for happiness may be genetic), our *upbringing*, our *life experience* and our *personality*; but by living positively we can expand our happiness potential. (Above material drawn from **http://news.bbc.co.uk/1/hi/programmes/happiness, 30/4/06.**)

Steven Reiss distinguishes between 'feel-good' happiness and 'value-based' happiness:

- 'Feel-good' happiness is 'sensation-based' happiness (pursuing pleasures that give us kicks); it is short-lived and gets harder to replicate.

- 'Value-based' happiness is what we experience when our lives have meaning and purpose. It involves a 'spiritual source of satisfaction' that comes from living our deeper values.

- 'Value-based' happiness is the great leveller. We can achieve it whatever our status or condition in life. The poor can be as happy as the rich, because true happiness comes from living in line with our values. (The article goes on to offer the 'Reiss profile' to help us identify 'The 16 keys to happiness'.)[19]

'The best you can do with positive emotion is you can get people to live at the top of their range. So I think you have got about 10–15% leverage, but you can't take a grouch and make him giggle all the time.'

Professor Martin Seligman, University of Pennsylvania

Professor Seligman's work indicates several things.

- People who win large amounts on the lottery eventually return to their previous level of happiness; people who become paraplegic after an accident do recover almost all their previous level of happiness.

- There are positive psychology 'exercises' we can do which can increase our long-term happiness level:

  - One of the most successful exercises was '**Three Blessings'**, in which people write down three things that went well for them at the end of each day.

  - Another was writing (and delivering personally) a **'Gratitude Letter'** to somebody who had done something for us that we had appreciated.

---

18 Professor Ed Diener University of Illinois as reported in
http://news.bbc.co.uk/1/hi/programmes/happiness and
http://newsvote.bbc.co.uk/mpapps/pagetools/print/news.bbc.co.uk/1/
programmes/happiness

19 'Secrets of Happiness', Steven Reiss, *Psychology Today*,
http://psychologytoday.co./articles

my work options

my finances

my relationships

my learning

my health and wellbeing

my leisure

my spirituality

my work options
my finances
my relationships
my learning
my health and wellbeing
my leisure
my spirituality

– The third is using our **'signature strength'** (a skill or a quality that 'marks us out', that we are particularly strong in and proud of) in an entirely new way. For example, if we have a particular sporting skill we use to participate in sport, we might look to turning that into coaching mode and working with a disadvantaged group to develop their skills and performance in our specialist sport.

The three exercises described have been used in work involving many people and have been shown to boost longer-term happiness levels. Why not build them into your life planning?

You can learn more about signature strengths and indeed happiness by visiting Professor Seligman's website at www.authentichappiness.sas.upenn.edu.

Activity 3.5

Understanding happiness

So, where are you with the subject of happiness? Consider the components of happiness listed below and rate your satisfaction with each in your current phase of life and career.

Use a rating of:

1 – **not as good as I would like, some work to be done**
2 – **OK but could be better**
3 – **good, very happy with this in my life**

■ The breadth, strength and depth of relationships in my life. ☐

■ Giving and receiving support from other people. ☐

■ Finding 'meaning' in my life from some source. ☐

■ Having goals in my life that are aligned with my values. ☐

■ Being involved in activities that are aligned with my values. ☐

■ What do I realise as a result of my reflections on relationships? What will I do as a result of these realisations?

_____

_____

_____

_____

_____

■ What do I realise as a result of my reflections on happiness?
What will I do as a result of these realisations?

_____

_____

_____

_____

_____

[end activity]

Other sections of this book which link with these themes are Theme 5, 'My health and wellbeing' and Theme 7, 'My spirituality'.

Finding out more

Web resources

- If you see yourself as a baby boomer, then you could explore www.babyboomerbistro.org.uk. This has been set up by Age Concern

- Try a web search on 'relationships and happiness' and 'relationships and health'

- Do a web search into the work of Professor Andrew Oswald and the links between politics and happiness

- *The Oldie* magazine has its own chat room for the over 50s www.theoldie.co.uk, as has www.idf50.co.uk/clubhouse

- www.employersforwork-lifebalance.org.uk

- www.familycaregiversonline.com
- www.inmyprime.co.uk
- www.sandwichgeneration.com
- Numerous diagnostic tools can be found at www.authentichappiness.com. You may in particular be interested in using the 'Satisfaction with life' scale, the 'Close relationships' questionnaire and 'Approaches to happiness' questionnaire

- www.realage.com is helpful on happiness and health.

- For more information please visit www.fiftyforward.co.uk

Action plans

Reviewing your reflections on your sources of support:

■ What range of people do you have in your support system?

_____

_____

_____

■ Are too many of your 'eggs in the one basket'? _____

■ Where are the gaps?

_____

_____

_____

■ What would it take to fill them?

_____

_____

_____

■ What will you do about what you have identified?

_____

_____

_____

my work options
my finances
my relationships
my learning
my health and wellbeing
my leisure
my spirituality

my work options
my finances
my relationships
my learning
my health and wellbeing
my leisure
my spirituality

On the basis of your reflections on your current relationships and the support you need and receive, on sources of happiness, as well as the other information you have surveyed in this section, write in what you would like more of, less of and what you would like to keep the same in your life right now.

MORE OF…	LESS OF…	KEEP THE SAME

Choose three that you would like to start working on right now:

1. _____

2. _____

3. _____

> 'It's difficult to say what has been the most important lesson from my lifetime but I would say life has taught me that appearances can be deceptive and one should not rush to judgement. That everybody has a value and a place in the great scheme of things. What matters is not what you own but what you have achieved, what sort of person you are and how you are able to relate to others. To love and be loved is perhaps the most important thing in life.'
>
> *Frances in her 60s*

my learning

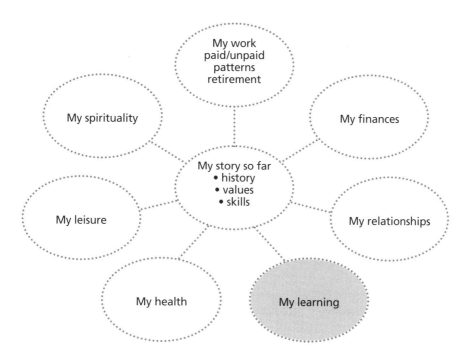

> 'Since 50 I have taken various courses in IT including spreadsheets, Sage and desktop publishing. My digital camera is a godsend. I use my computer to transcribe music. I never learned to play an instrument, so my computer allows me to be creative in this area.'
>
> *Janet, in her 60s*

Introduction

Most people like learning new things. We will all need to continue learning for the whole of our lives if we wish to avoid rusting away or becoming increasingly out of touch or left behind.

Sadly, some people are put off learning because of unfortunate experiences at school. However, it is vitally important to remember that we were very young then, possibly badly taught, and this was only 'formal' learning. It has been estimated that 85% of everything we learn is learnt outside of schools, colleges and training courses.

It is interesting to note that over 50s taking part in government training programmes are more committed and achieve better results than younger people, although starting with a lower level of formal qualifications.

Ask yourself what have you learned which is new to you:

■ Today?

_____

_____

■ In the past week?

_____

_____

■ In the past month?

_____

_____

How many of these things have you learned formally and how many have you learned by yourself, from being with friends or colleagues or from the media (TV, papers, radio, magazines, internet, etc.)?

Many people planning for the second half of their lives have *learning* high on their agenda. It could be learning about different places, different cultures, a new sport or hobby, new skills. It could be about developing new interests – genealogy, photography, working an allotment, working for a charity or community group.

> *'Taking up my guitar again after 30 years and joining a band has been a most rewarding experience.'*
>
> Chris Read, in his 60s

> *'I'm doing my PhD out of interest in the subject (Social Ethics) and because I have become addicted to study and also I greatly enjoy the contact with people in the class in their 20s.'*
>
> Mary, in her 70s, pursuing her second doctorate

This theme is designed to give you more insight into:

• How you learn and what motivates you to continue learning

• The way you personally learn – your preferred learning style

• The different learning methods that are available to you.

It will help you to understand and develop the skills you need to improve your own learning and performance.

Being a successful learner

This is a question that a great deal of research has tried to answer. Why is it that sometimes the learning we undertake fails dramatically, while other times we succeed? There are several answers to this question but all of them contain one element in common – motivation!

Our attitude to our own learning is all-important. If we don't take charge of our own development, no one else will! Therefore, it's vital that we are motivated and willing to learn.

Become a motivated learner

Research suggests that the following factors need to be in place if learning is to be successful:

• **Access and opportunity:** you need to be able to tap into the sources and resources appropriate to what you want to learn – these may be formal or informal, tutor led or self directed.

• **Information/guidance:** you need to be clear about *what* you want to learn – and have the support and guidance necessary, in order to learn it.

• **Purpose:** be clear what you want to get out of, or achieve from, your learning. Have goals to aim for.

• **Relevance:** it will help to recognise why the learning is important, how you will use it in your career or your life.

my work options

my finances

my relationships

my learning

my health and wellbeing

my leisure

my spirituality

- **Affordable:** this doesn't mean simply *financially* affordable, but affordable in terms of time, resources, etc.

- **Rewarded/celebrated:** we all need recognition for our achievements, whether it is in the form of qualification, monetary reward or simply positive feedback; without it, our motivation may slip.

Each of these elements is important, and a failure to learn in the past can often be traced back to a problem in one of these areas. Pause for a moment to think of any learning you've sought or undertaken in your life that did not work out; perhaps a course you didn't complete, or a school subject you weren't good at. Were any of the above six factors missing?

Motivation comes when we are committed to doing something; when we can see it makes sense, when we can see a return for our efforts, when we want it badly. 'Ownership' is a key word in learning and development. When you 'own' your own development, when you take responsibility for achieving things and are keen to progress, when you choose to work at it, when you are hungry for the benefits it can bring, you are highly likely to succeed. Each of us will work hard at the things we value and for which we can see 'pay-offs'. Pay-offs are not necessarily material gains; they could be greater self-confidence and self-satisfaction, a sense of achievement or new status.

Why is it important to go on learning as we get older?

Learning:

- Keeps our mind sharp and active

- Improves memory and helps keep our brain smart and active

- Increases self-confidence and optimism

- Can maintain our sense of 'advancement' rather than 'decline'

- Offers an inexpensive way to try something new

- Can save us money as we learn to 'do it ourselves'

- Gives us a feeling of accomplishment

- Helps us meet people who share our interests

- Can add to our social life and build new contacts

- Builds on skills we already have

- Offers us an opportunity to learn a new skill or trade and increase our income

- Gives us a new interest that we can share with family and friends, and can actually be fun!

Do you know?

- National Adult Learning Survey (2005) showed that 73% of adults had participated in education and training in the previous year. (We like to learn!)

- Any adult without a Level 2 qualification can get free tuition for a qualification up to that level across the UK from 2007.

- Older adults, in general, have the lowest level of formal qualifications. They are the least likely age group to volunteer for training, and the least likely to be offered training by their employers.

- Participation in training declines progressively with age, increasing the risk that individuals become unemployable. Although the Government's Skills Strategy guarantees free learning for full Level 2 qualifications and basic skills, and half of those without Level 2 qualifications are over 50, this age group are seriously under represented in this provision. However, the over 50's who do continue to train (generally those who are already better qualified) are much more likely to remain in the workforce.

- The workplace itself is becoming an ever-more important driver for learning. The number of people strongly agreeing to the statement 'my job requires that I keep learning new things' has consistently moved upwards since 1992: rising from 26% in 1992 to 30% in 2001 and then to 35% in 2006.

- The number strongly agreeing to the statement 'my job requires that I help my colleagues to learn new things' rose from 27% in 2001 to 32% in 2006.

- More older people are also choosing to participate in education and learn new skills, including the use of computers and the internet. In 2002, 51% of those aged 60–69 in England and Wales were engaged in some form of learning – as opposed to 47% in 1997.

- More retired people are studying, rising from 16% in 2006 to 19% in 2007.

- More than half (51.3%) of all the courses that people over 65 are taking relate to computer skills. The second most popular subject amongst older people is foreign languages, with over 1 in 10 (10.2%) of people aged over 55 engaged, compared to just 4.3% of people aged 17–44. These are the main findings of the latest research

my work options

my finances

my relationships

my learning

my health and wellbeing

my leisure

my spirituality

my work options

my finances

my relationships

my learning

my health and wellbeing

my leisure

my spirituality

from the National Institute of Adult Continuing Education (NIACE) (September 2007) into what older people learn.

- The number of over 75s engaged in learning has risen 5% to 15%, according to a 2007 poll.

- No longer the domain of only the young, the internet is fast becoming the hip hangout for older generations. A survey conducted in 2007 by the internet research firm Hitwise UK revealed that, any day now, 'silver surfers' (classified as internet users aged 55 and over) look likely to overtake the 35–44 age group as the group with the largest representation online.

- During a four-week period in 2007, those aged 55+ accounted for 22% of UK visits to all types of websites. Those aged 35–44 only just pipped them to the post, at 23.5%. Heather Hopkins, vice-president for research at Hitwise UK, says: 'Silver surfers show a particular fondness for travel, news and media websites, with these categories ranking higher among silver surfers [than for younger age groups]'.

- In one week, 27% of all UK visits to travel websites and 24% of visits to news and media websites were from those aged 55+.

- Silver surfers aren't just searching the web – they're creating the content as well. One of the most-viewed blogs on the ubiquitous YouTube site is run by 80-year-old Peter Oakley, **www.askgeriatric.com**, an 'internet grandad' who lives in rural Derbyshire and whose YouTube videos are watched by millions of fans around the world. He recently indulged in further stereotype-bashing by joining the Zimmers, the oldest gigging band in the world (their average age is 78), to record a version of The Who's 'My Generation' at Abbey Road studios.

A 2007 survey from Directgov in 2007 showed the top requirements for the internet for the over 50s were :

- To find out about local services aimed at older people – transport, leisure, learning, health

- To use webcams/video conferencing to stay in touch with friends, relatives

- For tracking pensions

- For planning for life after retirement

- To be able to use online services, regardless of physical situation or impairment

- To be able to claim for benefits

- To earn money through using skills online

- To receive objective and/or ethical financial advice.

Learning styles

We have talked about the theory of how people learn and what motivates them to continue learning. But how do *you*, personally, learn? We are all individuals and each of us has our own personal style or way of learning. Some of the material that follows has been inspired by, and adapted from, the work of Janet Hagberg and Richard Leider in their book, *Inventurers: Excursions in Life and Career Renewal*, Perseus Books, New York, 1978.

The following activity will help you identify and think about your own learning style. It will also help you to understand how you learn best, and will show you ways in which your style may differ from other people's styles.

Before you complete this questionnaire it is important to know that each learning style has its advantages and disadvantages. There is no 'best' style – all of them are equally valid, and each has its strengths and shortfalls. Almost all of us use *all* these learning styles at different times, but it is helpful to know if we have a predilection towards (or away from) any particular style, to allow us to learn in the most effective way.

Activity 4.1

What is my learning style?

For each of the following statements, decide whether the statement is:

1 – Not like you
2 – Somewhat like you
3 – Most like you

Circle the option that you think best describes you.
For the moment ignore the letter at the end of each statement.

	Not like me	Somewhat like me	Most like me
■ I work systematically on those subjects I don't enjoy, as well as on those I do. [L]	1	2	3
■ I check through everything I write to ensure its flow and accuracy. [L]	1	2	3
■ I pay great attention to detail in all I do. [L]	1	2	3
■ I like to understand how things work and how ideas have been developed. [L]	1	2	3
■ I enjoy solving problems and posing new questions. [L]	1	2	3
■ I like finishing one task before undertaking another. [L]	1	2	3
■ I am a good critic, asking searching questions and raising doubts. [L]	1	2	3
■ I prefer to work through problems for myself. [L]	1	2	3
■ I like to make lists, work out timetables and have clear action plans. [L]	1	2	3
■ I prefer to listen to ideas rather than talk. [L]	1	2	3
■ I re-work any project until I get it absolutely right. [L]	1	2	3
■ I stick to timetables and action plans I have made. [L]	1	2	3
■ I learn best by studying things for myself. [L]	1	2	3
■ I like reading for ideas and coming to my own conclusions. [L]	1	2	3
■ I would not describe my approach to work or learning as systematic. [I]	1	2	3
■ I like to spend a lot of time just thinking. [I]	1	2	3

my work options

my finances

my relationships

my learning

my health and wellbeing

my leisure

my spirituality

my work options
my finances
my relationships
my learning
my health and wellbeing
my leisure
my spirituality

	Not like me	Somewhat like me	Most like me
■ I like making connections between different topics, enjoying seeing how ideas link together. [I]	1	2	3
■ I can spend a long time thinking about work without actually getting down to it. [I]	1	2	3
■ I prefer thinking and talking to written assignments. [I]	1	2	3
■ I like to find original, new ways of completing and presenting work. [I]	1	2	3
■ I like to work in bursts of energy. [I]	1	2	3
■ I like to float ideas around with other people. [I]	1	2	3
■ I am comfortable working without timetables or plans. [I]	1	2	3
■ I enjoy coming up with new questions and alternatives. [I]	1	2	3
■ I would rather work from, and produce, creative diagrams than straightforward lists. [I]	1	2	3
■ I don't like detail, I prefer seeing the whole picture. [I]	1	2	3
■ I enjoy challenging ideas. [I]	1	2	3
■ I like daydreaming, for me it's fruitful. [I]	1	2	3
■ I like a clear purpose and direction. [P]	1	2	3
■ I like planning my work. [P]	1	2	3
■ I like to know exactly what is required or expected before starting a project. [P]	1	2	3
■ I know what is important to me and what I want to achieve. [P]	1	2	3
■ I like working on my own. [P]	1	2	3
■ I like to get on with a task and not be side-tracked by new approaches or alternatives. [P]	1	2	3
■ I respect deadlines and am impatient with those who don't. [P]	1	2	3

	Not like me	Somewhat like me	Most like me
■ I am usually very well organised. [P]	1	2	3
■ I think in advance about equipment and resources I need for work. [P]	1	2	3
■ I use lists, charts and graphs that give data rather than attempt to produce works of art. [P]	1	2	3
■ I enjoy getting down to work. [P]	1	2	3
■ I read instructions carefully and work methodically, I like timetables and agendas. [P]	1	2	3
■ I enjoy finishing a task. [P]	1	2	3
■ I get bored easily and enjoy moving on to new things. [E]	1	2	3
■ I enjoy working in groups. [E]	1	2	3
■ I am not interested in detail. [E]	1	2	3
■ I learn by talking through ideas with other people. [E]	1	2	3
■ I like getting on with things; doing is more attractive than planning. [E]	1	2	3
■ I like variety; I like flitting from one task to another. [E]	1	2	3
■ When I'm interested I get totally involved, when I'm not I shy away from topics. [E]	1	2	3
■ I like skip reading; trying to absorb everything is not my style. [E]	1	2	3
■ I enjoy writing freely, letting the ideas flow rather than thinking things through first. [E]	1	2	3
■ I don't read through or check my work once it's completed. [E]	1	2	3
■ I like asking lots of questions to find out all I need to know. [E]	1	2	3
■ I like new ideas and approaches. [E]	1	2	3
■ I like to take life as it comes and be spontaneous. [E]	1	2	3

my work options

my finances

my relationships

my learning

my health and wellbeing

my leisure

my spirituality

my work options

my finances

my relationships

my learning

my health and wellbeing

my leisure

my spirituality

Total up your scores for each of statements marked L, then each statement marked I, then P and finally E – enter your scores in each category here:

You scored _____ as a Logical learner. (L)

You scored _____ as an Imaginative learner. (I)

You scored _____ as a Practical learner. (P)

You scored _____ as an Enthusiastic learner. (E)

[end activity]

Your highest score indicates your *dominant* learning style – the one that has got you the best learning results in your life so far. We each have the capacity to extend our learning style but, over the years, tend to stick to what works best for us. Remember, there is no one 'best' style – each style has its advantages and disadvantages.

Below, you will find a description of the characteristics of each style of learning. Look at your scores and then check out the descriptions below. Do these descriptions mirror the ways in which you choose to learn – or do not choose to learn?

Logical learners:

Advantages	Disadvantages
organise work well	can need too much information and over-elaborate
are keen to understand things and make links	can get bogged down in the theory
are curious; keen to learn; enjoy problems	can be reluctant to try new approaches
plan well, and work systematically	can be set in their ways and uncreative
are precise and thorough	tend not to use others as support
like debate, are good critics	tend not to be adventurous
will rework things and iron out errors	work from the head rather than the heart
	trust only logic

Imaginative learners:

Advantages	Disadvantages
are able to see new ways of working	are not attracted to detail; like to see the 'big picture'
produce creative solutions	can be slow to actually get down to work
can see long-term implications and consequences	can be uncritical of ideas
are unhurried; tend to be easy going and unflappable	can be too easy going and unassertive
listen to others and share ideas	tend to work in bursts of energy, rather than systematically
see links between topics and concepts	can be somewhat disorganised
will work in novel and artistic ways	
are able to pinpoint important questions	

Practical learners:

Advantages	Disadvantages
work well on their own	expect others to be clear and thorough; can be impatient with those who are not
are good at setting goals and making action plans	believe own way is the best and only right way
know how to find out what they need to know	tend not to use others for support
are good at applying theories	can be preoccupied with the details and fail to see the 'big picture'
get things done on time	
are single minded, not easily distracted	can lack imagination
are organised, and good time managers	can be more interested in the completion, than the quality of work
are thorough; absorb information well	
have organised filing/retrieval systems	

Enthusiastic learners:

Advantages	Disadvantages
will throw themselves into things that interest them	may not be keen on planning and organising
will work well with others; likely to use and give support	can be difficult to motivate when the topic does not interest them
will try new ideas	likely to take on too many things at once
work quickly and get others enthusiastic	not likely to rework what they produce, will be keen to move on to the next topic
enjoy variety and excitement	likely to work to priorities and to leave things to the last minute
will question and challenge; enjoy talking about ideas	
like skip reading or writing freely	can have difficulty in focusing

We often expect others to learn in the same way as ourselves. Our style works for us, but different styles work for different people. *Logicals* are likely to have the most difficulty when working with *Enthusiasts* and vice versa. *Practicals* and *Imaginatives* may not feel comfortable when starting to work with each other.

We all have the capacity to develop the other styles; our dominant one is simply the one that we have used most so far and (possibly) which we find most suitable.

We need to understand the features of different styles so we can work with other people in a style that makes sense to them. When we can work in other styles, people feel that we are on their 'wavelength',

and if we are part of a team the team will be able to work more effectively.

If you are working through this book with a friend or acquaintance, you may find that the other person learns in a different way to you. If you understand this, then there can be real advantages in working with someone with a different style: they will bring a different slant to a task, which could be illuminating. On the other hand, it could be frustrating, if you don't understand why! Work with them as, with patience, you may learn something to your advantage.

These learning styles also have implications when you decide which is the best learning method for you.

my work options
my finances
my relationships
my learning
my health and wellbeing
my leisure
my spirituality

my work options
my finances
my relationships
my learning
my health and wellbeing
my leisure
my spirituality

Learning methods

It's important to realise that there are many methods of learning available to us, and if we have an understanding of which method suits us best, our learning will be far more successful.

Below, you will find a variety of learning methods – most of which don't include a blackboard As you read through, think about the methods which work best for you. You might also ask yourself which methods sit most comfortably with you if you are trying to help someone else to learn.

• Coaching

Coaching allows people to develop skills in a controlled, yet flexible, environment. It is not about being 'taught', but about being helped to learn through experience. This type of learning draws on the experience of the coach to guide and assist the learner through the problems and pitfalls of a task in a real work situation. He or she will also help the learner to review tasks, to improve future performance.

• Mentoring

A mentor is an experienced and trusted advisor: a manager, a colleague or any skilled and experienced person. A mentor can give useful advice and insights, and can also set informal development tasks to improve our knowledge. A learner and a mentor will, over time, build a relationship based on trust and focused on the learner's development. This is a role that becomes increasingly popular with age and some companies are encouraging older workers to engage in this, prior to their leaving or going part time.

• Shadowing

One of the most popular traditional methods of learning is to observe, or shadow, someone who is proficient whilst he or she works. As long as the learning is monitored and reviews and standards are applied, this can be a very useful way of learning specific skills.

• Courses

This is the most traditional way of learning, by being led by a specialist in a particular topic. There are many different traditional education and training courses available to you. The learndirect website will be able to give you all the information you need on this.

• Networking

Networking is about making and maintaining effective contacts. This encourages you to consider and involve others in your learning activities. For example, by lending someone a copy of a report, sending them a website reference or by passing on some useful tips, you can then expect to receive similar support yourself.

• Group or team sessions

This is an effective way of learning, which offers excellent opportunities for team building and team development. It is also a great way of learning from other people and sharing your own expertise.

• Flexible/open/eLearning

This involves working through a programme in book or manual, or on the internet, mainly on your own, but possibly coming together with others at certain times – either face-to-face or using internet forums. The great advantage of this approach is that it allows you to be self motivating and self managing. It also allows you to study where, when and in the way you choose. Depending on your learning style, however, you could also feel quite isolated, so you might want to link up with a fellow learner.

Activity 4.2

Which learning method is best for you? (1)

Thinking about the above sources or methods of learning, answer the following questions.

■ Which best suits your learning style?

_____

_____

_____

_____

_____

_____

■ Which might be the best source of your next piece of learning?

_____

_____

_____

_____

_____

_____

■ What do you see as your next learning requirements in terms of your life or your career?

_____

_____

_____

_____

_____

_____

■ What do you need to do to make this happen?

_____

_____

_____

_____

_____

_____

[end activity]

Activity 4.3

Which learning method is best for you? (2)

Read through the table and decide which learning method you think suits you best. Remember, the ideas above are only suggestions. There is no right or wrong way to learn and you shouldn't be put off from learning in any way you wish.

Mastering new ways of learning will broaden your abilities and help you accelerate your development.

	LOGICALS	IMAGINATIVES	PRACTICALS	ENTHUSIASTS
coaching	like to have time to absorb things and ask detailed questions at their own pace	like to have an opportunity to really talk through things in a relaxed way	like direct help and full attention, without waiting for others to catch up	benefit from a structured approach to learning and having to demonstrate understanding or competence
mentoring	like an opportunity to talk through things in detail and without pressure	like to talk through things in an unhurried way and to bounce ideas off colleagues	benefit from talking through ideas and plans when receiving feedback	benefit from formulating ideas and then explaining them to other people to receive feedback
shadowing	like to analyse in detail, are good at observation and benefit from doing something that is real and not theoretical	would benefit from watching real behaviour	like an action-based, hands-on approach to learning	like to learn from activity
courses	like to learn from systematic training but dislike ambiguous situations	would benefit from listening to views from a wider group but dislike large groups	like to learn only if it is relevant and would benefit from taking a different perspective	like to learn in large groups
networking	like to develop systems but would benefit from having to make them happen	like to set up supportive relationships and enjoy helping others	like to develop their own contacts for mutual benefit	like to make new relationships and to have a wide circle of colleagues
group or team sessions	would benefit from listening to others and working as part of a team	like to talk and listen in a team about ideas and concepts and like to be creative	would benefit from working with team members	like to learn by talking with others but would benefit from having assignments agreed by the team
flexible/open/ elearning	like to work at own pace and to work thoroughly	like to have time to reflect without being pressurised to complete a task	like to work on their own without the distractions of working with others	would benefit from taking time to think things through for themselves

[end activity]

One of the most important stages in the learning process is reviewing the learning experience. Taking time to do this will ensure we stay on target. Often the best source of review can come from the people around us, who can give us their perspective on how we are doing.

Finding out more

It would be especially useful for you to discuss your thoughts on this theme with a friend, to enable you to compare learning styles and to explore with them the implications for your learning.

Contact learndirect for information on 0800 100 900 to talk in confidence and to get advice on opportunities for learning.

Summary

You have:

- Discovered your preferred learning style and identified its strengths and weaknesses

- Explored the different methods of learning and identified which are the ones that fit best with your learning style.

'The mind is not a vessel to be filled, but a fire to be kindled.'

Plutarch, c. 46–120 AD

Web resources

- Try the following websites for ideas on keeping your brain active every day.
  www.bellydoc.com/articles/article7.htm
  www.sharpbrains.com/blog/2007/04/03/brain-exercise-faqs
  www.sharpbrains.com/blog/category/brain-teasers.

- You can also do online learning for minimal or no cost through the University of the Third Age, www.u3a-info.co.uk.

- If you want to exercise your brain by learning more about using the internet and email try www.silverhairs.co.uk – that will lead you to many other sites.

- www.hairnet.org was the first dedicated computer and internet training scheme for the over 50s – it is now called Digital Unite.

- Try searching the web for phrases like 'learning opportunities', 'lifelong learning', 'learning for seniors UK'.

- For more information please visit www.fiftyforward.co.uk

Action plans

Review what you have worked on in this theme. Now, in the table below write in what you want more of, less of and what you would like to keep the same in your life right now.

	MORE OF...	LESS OF...	KEEP THE SAME
Formal learning			
Informal learning			

my work options

my finances

my relationships

my learning

my health and wellbeing

my leisure

my spirituality

my work options

my finances

my relationships

my learning

my health and wellbeing

my leisure

my spirituality

'My plans are to do something new every year. It might be to learn a new skill, take on a new appointment, teach someone a skill or contribute to society in some way.'

Graham, in his 50s

'(I will…) take up water colour painting as a prelude to retirement and anything else which appeals to me. I may join a belly-dancing class in the autumn… to keep challenging myself and enjoying life.'

Janet, in her 60s

Notes

my health and wellbeing

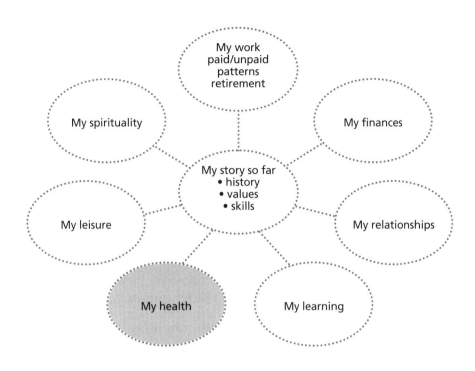

> 'Life expectancy at age 65 in the UK has reached its highest level ever for both men and women. Men aged 65 can expect to live a further 16.6 years and women a further 19.4 years if mortality rates remain the same as they were in 2003–05.'
>
> *www.statistics.gov.uk*

Introduction

The good news is the over 50s are living longer than any previous generation.

Life expectancy is increasing year by year. In 2008 it was announced that for a married couple of around 60 there is almost a 50% chance that one of them will reach 90.

Life expectancy at birth increased by almost a decade in the first 50 years of the NHS. In 1948, 40% of people died before reaching pensionable age, this was reduced to 7% by 1996.

The gerontologist, John Grimley Evans has said, 'we are spending a longer time living and a shorter time dying'.

Our longevity and our level of wellbeing during it will obviously be key factors in our planning: career, financial and indeed all our other planning. Feeling fit, well and able to pursue our life and career choices is surely a cornerstone of an enriched second half of our life. Even allowing for the sudden onset of illness, accidents and other unpredictable life events, by adopting healthy habits and lifestyles we can expect many fruitful, rewarding decades ahead at 50+. Some of the longevity we enjoy will be a gift of our genes. Our family history, the medical conditions which afflicted our ancestors and the life spans that resulted will have an influence on our lives but, as we will see, it is likely to be our lifestyles and health choices that most greatly influence our health experience and longevity.

Longevity, of course, has to be evaluated against *quality of life*. When jogging first became popular the cynics would joke, 'People who jog everyday can expect to live some seven years longer than people who don't. Do you know what they do with those extra seven years? THEY JOG!'

One scientist, whose work suggests that reduced calorie intake can significantly increase life span, demonstrates his faith in his research by living on 1,500 calories a day. Others might decide that sacrificing superb food and wine over decades to add time to one's old age is not a price worth paying. Surely, therefore, the ideal is to design a lifestyle that allows us to moderately enjoy the good things of life, whilst maintaining that level of health and wellbeing that leaves us able to pursue all our wishes in our work, relationships, community and leisure lives. The keys to staying healthy and enjoying the second half of our lives are generally recognised as being:

- Diet
- Exercise
- Work
- Life enhancers.

'The secret of staying young is to live honestly, eat slowly, and lie about your age.'

Lucille Ball

Do you know?

- Taking half-an-hour of exercise each day, not drinking more than 14 units of alcohol per week, eating five servings of fruit and vegetables daily and not smoking, can add up to 14 years to our longevity. (Research by University of Cambridge and Medical Research Council reported on **http://news.bbc.co.uk**, 2008)
- In the ten years up to 2006, the number of adults in the UK dying from heart disease fell by 44% thanks to improved diets, reduced smoking and increased commitment to taking exercise. (British Heart Foundation, 2006)

- Our 60s are a particularly significant time in health terms. There are real gains to be made from monitoring health symptoms and having regular medical checks. A health checklist for those in their 60s is available from **health@thirdage.com**.
- Some studies suggest that genes are responsible for up to 50% of our changes in mental functions and 35% of our physiological changes as we age and that longevity itself is 25–35% inheritable. This leaves plenty of room to make a difference through diet, exercise and regular medical checks. (Source; *Living better, living longer – the secrets of healthy aging*, a special health report from Harvard Medical School, 2008)
- People age at different rates and so do different organs in the body. Our lung capacity declines, on average, by about 40% between the ages of 20 and 70. Our heart's maximum oxygen capacity declines by roughly 10% in men and 7.5% in women for *each decade of adult life*.
- Inactivity causes muscle mass to drop 22% for women and 23% for men between ages 30 and 70. Bone loss outstrips bone build-up starting about age 35. Kidneys gradually lose their efficiency. (Source: Baltimore Longitudinal Study of Aging)

The good news is that all the declines mentioned above can be offset, or delayed by adopting healthy practices.

- More good news is that a glass of wine a day could help to delay dementia in people with mild cognitive impairment (MCI), a new study claims. MCI is a transitional phase between normal ageing and dementia and is evident from mild memory or cognitive problems and no significant disability. Scientists found that people with MCI who had one drink of alcohol a day, mostly wine, developed dementia at an 85% slower rate than people with mild cognitive impairment who never drank alcohol. Higher levels of drinking were not found to have a beneficial effect on dementia progression. (University of Bari study by Solfrizzi and Panza)
- Four hours of brisk walking per week can prolong life by four to five years (Copenhagen City Heart Study).
- A Future Foundation report commissioned in 2007 by intone, a Help the Aged subsidiary, shows the over 50s taking personal fitness just as seriously as

my work options

my finances

my relationships

my learning

my health and wellbeing

my leisure

my spirituality

younger generations did 50 years ago. They take part in the same amount of sport as 25-year-olds did in 1957; when time for hobbies is added on, the over 50s spend almost three hours a week more on leisure now than their counterparts did 50 years ago.

- The same survey showed that people in their 60s and 70s generally feel in good health, and that there are only modest differences between that group and those in their 40s and 50s in terms of control and quality of life. People over 60 actually report feeling more in control than those in their 40s and 50s.

- For some people, things actually improve after the age of 60. 70 is becoming the new 50 in terms of active healthy ageing. There are few differences between men and women on this.

- According to a 2008 survey by Saga/Populus, focusing on the health of the over 50s in the UK, 38% of those over 65 exercise every day (compared to 29% of the 50–54s); 76% try to eat the recommended amounts of fruit and vegetable daily. 65% claim to be sexually active (46% at least once a week), and 85% find sex is less pressurised after 50; 70% say it is more fulfilling than in younger years.

- The *New England Journal of Medicine*, August 2007, reported research by Dr Lindau of the University of Chicago, which indicated that 73% of those in the study aged between 57 and 64 were sexually active, 53% of those between 65 and 74, and 26% of those between 75 and 85.

General fitness

- The UK is one of the healthier countries: 73% of 70 to 79-year-olds, and 89% of 40 to 49-year-olds, feel in good or very good health. Those aged 60–79 years predominantly describe themselves as being in fair, good or very good health.

- Some care homes for the elderly are beginning to explore the potential of the Nintendo Wii games machine for providing mental and physical exercise for some of their less active residents.

- Women who began walking a mile a day after the age of 65 are half as likely to have died of heart disease or cancer compared with those who didn't. (*Journal of American Medical Association*, 2003)

- A study of 800 older men in Holland associated regular cycling with a 29% reduction in the death rate.

- Gardeners who spend more than an hour a week on their hobby are less likely to die of a heart attack than people who don't.

- A study of more than 25,000 men and 7,000 women showed that staying moderately fit proves protective even when a person smokes, has high blood pressure, high cholesterol or other health problems. (*Journal of American Medical Association*, 1996)

- The fastest walkers in a Nurses' Health Study reduced their risk of a stroke by 40% over the slowest walkers.

- An extensive study, reported in the 2006 *Journal of Urology,* indicated that those who exercised regularly enjoyed a lower risk of erectile dysfunction than those who exercised less often.

- The people who tend to live longest in the world are likely to live in communities where people walk miles everyday, frequently uphill. This pattern of life strengthens hearts, lungs, joints and muscles and living to 100 in not uncommon in these circumstances.

- The monks of the monastery of Mount Athos in Greece are amongst the healthiest group of people in the world, being described as 'extraordinarily disease free'. They have a greatly reduced incidence, compared with other people of their age group (between age 50 and 104) in other parts of the world, of cancers of the oesophagus, the bowel, the stomach, the intestines, the bladder, and the prostate. They also have reduced cardiovascular disease, a complete absence of Alzheimer's, and great longevity. This is believed to be the result of their spiritual life (they own nothing and know they never will), their serenity and living on a diet that is very similar to that of the traditional Greek peasant. They have a diet rich in fruit, vegetables, olive oil, bread, cereals, legumes, with occasional fish and no meat at all. They eat pulses; eat fresh (never anything which is out of season); eat small (meals last only 20 minutes to prevent over-eating); eat light (oil-based cooking one day – water-based the next; They have little salt and no butter or cream and have no processed food, but make much use of herbs and spices to provide flavour. The monks are also celibate. (Helena Smith 'The Mount Athos plan; lifestyle secrets of the world's healthiest people', *The Guardian*)

- Recent research suggests that having a positive approach to life brings benefits of longevity. A study at Yale University showed that older adults who had positive thoughts about ageing, lived seven-and-a-half years longer than those who did not. They had a greater 'will to live', thinking that the positive benefits of ageing far outweighed the potential hardships. This was even more important than the additional four years of life resulting from low blood pressure and cholesterol, and the one-to-three year gains in life expectancy of people who have not smoked and exercise regularly.

- The population of Okinawa, Japan, enjoy great longevity and healthy old age. The contributors to this include diet, genes, exercise and optimism. Research finds that Okinawans have a remarkably positive outlook on life. 'They have strong coping skills and a deep sense of spirituality, meaning and purpose. Positive outlook in the Okinawans is thought to explain their reduced risk of dementia.'(www.about.com)

- Research by Dr Thomas Hess at North Carolina University advises the avoidance of 'the stereotype threat'. Older people who focus more positively on life, who refuse to see themselves as old and in decline, who look 'for the good news rather than the bad', out-perform their more negative peers in a range of areas of their lives. (*Saga Magazine*, 2004)

- Laughter reduces stress and blood pressure, boosts our immune system and improves our social links. (www.helpguide.org)

- Research by The Study of Adult Development Unit at Harvard University, tracking adults over decades, indicates that those aged 50 can influence whether they will be 'happy– well' at 80, 'sad–sick' at 80, or dead before that, by addressing six areas of their lives: maintaining a normal weight; not smoking; having a stable relationship; drinking less alcohol; being adaptable; and taking regular exercise. (Peter Crookston, 'Why Older means Wiser', *Saga Magazine,* April 2004)

Optimism – is the glass half full or half empty?

- Grateful people – those who perceive gratitude as part of their personality rather than a temporary state of mind – have benefits over the less grateful, when it comes to health, according to research on gratitude. (http://psychology.ucdavis.edu/labs/emmons) Grateful people take better care of themselves and engage in more protective health behaviours such as regular exercise, a healthy diet and regular physical examinations.

- Work done by Drs Robert Emmons and Michael McCullough[20] indicated that those who focused on the positive things in life rather than the negative and were grateful, felt better about life, were more optimistic, more successful in achieving what they aimed for, were more helpful to other people, and had fewer physical symptoms.

- Tal Ben-Shahar teaches the most popular psychology course at Harvard University. Based on research and scientific evidence, he advises these four ways to live a happier life:

  – 'Give yourself permission to be human'; accept your emotions as part of life, which has downs a well as ups.

  – 'Simplify your life'; time-pressure, multi-tasking, being constantly available via new technology, over-committing, is like playing several pieces of our favourite music all at the same time; result: cacophony and hassle.

  – 'Exercise regularly'; regular, appropriate exercise has been shown to be as effective as taking anti-depressants. Exercise is natural and necessary and increases our self-esteem, our mental functioning, boosts our immune system, helps us sleep better, and can improve our sex life.

  – 'Focus on the positive'; make being optimistic and grateful a way of life; practising making gratitude a daily activity for a month is a great step towards making it a habit. (Tal Ben-Shahar (2007) 'Cheer up. Here's how…', *The Guardian*, December 2007)

- Nassim Nicholas Taleb, author of *The Black Swan*, advises us to 'embrace randomness' to remove the pressure of deadlines, time limits, and 'optimal' performance (the idea that everything we do has to be 'the best', or the hardest, or the longest, or the most challenging). He says that 'the pressure to be optimal', even in our enjoyment, produces pressure and distress. His view is that we are 'made to live life like firemen or cheetahs, with downtime for lounging (possibly meditating) between calls or attacks'. He believes we should 'inject unpredictability and surprise into our exercise, work, meditation, private encounters'… and that we should make 'our exercise of random length, avoid closely spaced appointments to make room for last-minute schemes, avoid rigid schedules, and enjoy just what we are meant to be – humans.' (Nassim Nicholas Taleb (2008), *Observer Health Magazine*, July 2008, author's views based on his book (2004) *Fooled by Randomness*: Penguin, UK, 2007)

- Grateful people tend to be more optimistic, a characteristic that researchers say boosts the immune

20 *The Psychology of Gratitude*, Oxford University Press, 2002

my work options

my finances

my relationships

my learning

my health and wellbeing

my leisure

my spirituality

system. 'There are some very interesting studies linking optimism to better immune function,' says Lisa Aspinwall, a psychology professor at the University of Utah. In one study, researchers comparing the immune systems of healthy, first-year law students, under stress, found that, by mid-term, students characterised as optimistic (based on survey responses) maintained higher numbers of blood cells that protect the immune system, compared with their more pessimistic classmates.

- Optimism also has a positive health impact on people with compromised health. In separate studies, patients with AIDS, as well as those preparing to undergo surgery, had better health outcomes when they maintained attitudes of optimism.

- In the last 75 years, IQs have increased by more than 20 points due (mainly) to improved childhood nutrition. Accessing information on the internet enhances our brain's performance. (www.thenakedscientists.com, 2007)

- Around ten hours of intensive mental exercise training over a six-week period can rejuvenate the thinking ability of the over 65s by the equivalent of 7 to 14 years. (*Daily Telegraph*, 8 September 2005

- In 1953 there were 200 centenarians in the UK. In 2006, there were around 10,000. By the year 2074, the number will be around 1.2 million. (Government Actuary's Department, 2006).

- Health and work are linked. The long-term unemployed are three times more likely to suffer long-term illness or disability than those in managerial and professional occupations. Those who have never worked are six times more likely to suffer. (Office for National Statistics, 2001 Census)

- A University of California study showed that people's immune systems weakened with the stress of unemployment. The immune system of those finding work showed a substantial recovery. (*Psychosomatic Medicine*, March 2007)

- Those out of work have poorer mental health than those in work. The unemployed make greater use of GPs and hospital services and require more medication. Those unemployed for more than a year experience eight times the amount of mental ill-health than do those in work. (*The Health and Work Handbook*, Faculty of Occupational Medicine, 2005)

- Older employees who work in low-stress jobs, with the hours they want, experience better health. (Centre for Retirement Research, USA, 2006)

- Work Fit, a lifestyle management programme

addressing diet and exercise offered by the Men's Health Forum in association with BT, was particularly successful in attracting older males. ('Older men, work and health', TAEN, 2008)

- 'Good work' has a beneficial effect on health. 'Good work' is that which offers 'safety, fairness, job security, personal fulfilment and job satisfaction, good communications, personal autonomy and a supportive environment.' (*Is work good for your health and wellbeing?* Department of Work and Pensions, 2006)

- Not all jobs are 'healthful' of course. Dr Hewett, of the Centre for Work–Life Policy, researches what she calls 'extreme jobs' – those that are fast-paced and involve long hours (more than 60 hours a week). These jobs can produce the kinds and levels of stress that cause 'burnout'. The 'stressors' she identifies are: rigidity with unpredictability; fast pace and tight deadlines; 24/7 availability to clients; constant travel; work-related events outside working hours; frustrating interruptions during the working day thanks to intrusive modern communications. (Valerie Grove (2008) 'Speed hazard; lead your life in the slow lane', *The Times*, March 2008)

- A study in the USA showed that mortality in the ten years following retirement was twice as high for those who stopped working at 55 than for those who did so at 65. (*British Medical Journal*, 2005)

- Working for more than 100 hours a year as a volunteer or in paid work, when working conditions are good, had a beneficial effect on the health of older workers. Working the number of hours they want in low-stress situations is most beneficial, though physically demanding jobs can benefit the physical health of older workers. (Centre for Retirement Research, USA, 2006)

- More people retire early due to ill-health that for any other reason ('*Older People, Work and Health*', TAEN, 2008)

- A report in the USA found that 90% of retirees get virtually no exercise and that more than 50% are totally sedentary. (www.thirdage.com)

- A Californian study focused on the value of sleep, which showed that the optimum number of hours appears to be seven. A six-year study showed that those who slept seven hours per night had the lowest rate of mortality; those who slept more than seven had the highest. Enough it seems is healthier than too much! (*The Observer Health Magazine*, July 2008)

my work options

my finances

my relationships

my learning

my health and wellbeing

my leisure

my spirituality

my work options

my finances

my relationships

my learning

my health and wellbeing

my leisure

my spirituality

> 'Today, 50 is closer to the middle of our life than to its end…there has been a shift from a 'closing down' expectation for the second half of life towards a more optimistic 'opening-of-new-doors' spirit of good times ahead.'
>
> *Martin Lloyd Elliott – psychologist*

> 'I find many things in life are easier now I am older and I am more relaxed and under less pressure. I think a positive attitude to life has a lot to do with good health and I am blessed with this. I have been surprised to find, in fact, how little has changed in my life; that old age is a continuum of everything that has gone before and that I remain the same person, just slower, more forgetful, less able to concentrate for long spells, a bit deaf etc.'
>
> *Mildred in her 80s*

Activity 5.1

Healthy living – what do I know?

Today there is a huge amount of coverage in the media of the latest health research and findings. We are bombarded by advice on what it takes to get and stay healthy. But how much do we KNOW of the details behind the advice and what do we DO about it?

■ Consider each of the statements below and circle the **T** if you believe it to be TRUE or the **F** if you decide it to be FALSE. The answers and sources of information on the internet are listed below.

1. Men can safely drink up to three pints of beer, or four shorts, or two large glasses of wine a day and women can drink up to two pints, or two large glasses of wine or four shorts or cocktails a day.   T   F

2. The UK recommended daily calorie intake is 2,550 for men and 1,940 for women.   T   F

3. Being overweight or obese is very likely to be damaging to health and wellbeing.   T   F

4. Being overweight is all due to our genetic makeup.   T   F

5. We should all know our Body Mass Index (BMI) to recognise whether we are overweight.   T   F

6. To stay healthy we should all eat at least five portions of fruit and vegetables every day (not including potatoes).   T   F

7. Saturated fats (found in dairy products, red meat, palm and coconut oils) and hydrogenated fats (found in fast food, types of margarines, commercial cakes and biscuits) should be avoided; monounsaturated and polyunsaturated fats (found in olive oil, some nut oils and oily fish) can be beneficial.   T   F

8. As long as we keep below the recommended daily calorie intake, it doesn't matter much what we eat.   T   F

9. Some carbohydrates (potatoes, especially fried, pizza, refined cereals, sugar, soft drinks, white bread, white rice) are to be eaten sparingly, while others (brown rice, whole grains, whole fruits, legumes, whole wheat products) are much more beneficial.   T   F

10. Protein is best obtained from fish, trimmed poultry, lean meat, eggs, beans, nuts, grains and a variety of vegetables.   T   F

11. Taking vitamin and other food supplements is essential.   T   F

Now check your answers…

How did you do?

1. False – these levels of intake are likely to take the drinkers above the safety limits recommended by the NHS (see **www.nhsdirect.nhs.uk**). However, recent revelations as to how those guidelines were established under Government pressure, without supportive research, has reopened the debate of what is 'safe'. Other countries have higher recommended alcohol levels.

2. True.

3. True – obesity significantly reduces life expectancy and is linked to a range of health problems. (See the 'Select Committee on Health – Third Report', **www.parliament.uk**, 2004.)

4. False – while there are links being established between certain genes and the likelihood of a person becoming obese, the most common cause of increasing obesity is still regarded as inappropriate diet and lack of exercise. (See information on obesity on **www.nhsdirect.nhs.uk**.)

5. True – it should be part of our health awareness – you can use the BMI Calculator on **www.eufic.org/article/en/rid/eufic-bmi-calculator** to check whether you are the right weight for your height.

6. True – take the 5-a-day Quiz on **www.nhsdirect.nhs.uk** (click **www.5aday.nhs.uk** to see what is meant by a portion).

7. True.

8. False – a balanced healthy diet requires more vegetables and less salt, sugar and saturated fats than a typical diet see **www.takelifeon.co.uk**.

9. True.

10. True.

11. False – we may only need these if our diet is deficient in any way or if we have a medical condition and they are prescribed. (See 'vitamins' on **www.nhsdirect.nhs.uk**.)

(Any data not otherwise accredited is based on the excellent *Living Better, Living Longer – the Secrets of Healthy Aging* – a special health report by the Harvard Medical School, available from **www.health.harvard.edu**.)

[end activity]

> '*In youth we learn, in old age we understand.*'
>
> *Mexican Proverb*

The benefits of exercise

> '*If there is anything close to a fountain of youth it is exercise. Given its proven benefits and low side-effect profile, if it were a pill everybody would be on it!*'
>
> *Dr Anne Fabiny, geriatrician and Assistant Professor of Medicine, Harvard Medical School*

We all 'know' that exercise is generally good – but what do you really know? Try this simple test!

my work options

my finances

my relationships

my learning

my health and wellbeing

my leisure

my spirituality

135

Activity 5.2

Use it or lose it

Again, consider each of the statements below and circle **T** for True or **F** for False after each statement. The following can result from building appropriate exercise into our daily life:

1.	Stronger heart and lungs	T	F
2.	Increased respect from other people	T	F
3.	Increase of 'good' and decrease of 'bad' cholesterol in our blood stream	T	F
4.	Increase in energy levels and feeling of refreshment resulting from increased intake of oxygen	T	F
5.	Appearing sexier	T	F
6.	Reduction in high blood pressure	T	F
7.	Improved sight and hearing	T	F
8.	Strengthening of muscles and bones	T	F
9.	Improvement in balance and coordination	T	F
10.	Reduced baldness	T	F
11.	Maintenance of healthy body weight	T	F
12.	Desire to eat more desserts	T	F
13.	Prevention and management of diabetes	T	F
14.	Improved mood	T	F
15.	Increase in libido	T	F
16.	Improved coping with pain, stress and depression	T	F
17.	Injury or worse	T	F
18.	Improvement in how we look and feel	T	F
19.	Reduced risk of certain cancers	T	F
20.	Better sleep	T	F
21.	Longer life	T	F

How did you do?

In fact research suggests that all the results of regular exercise listed are True – except four of them:

- – Improved sight and hearing
- – Appearing sexier
- – Cure for baldness
- – Increased respect from other people

…which seem to be as yet unproven. Still, it seems that exercise is full of promise!

[end activity]

Research then has shown that all the benefits identified as True can result from introducing a moderate amount of exercise into our daily life (see www.mayoclinic.com) apart from 'injury or worse'! That is included to ensure that we do not unwisely move too quickly from a life of low physical activity to one of energetic exercise. Please note the following points.

- Embarking on an exercise programme in the second half of our lives should be done with caution! **Advice should be taken from our doctors and if given the go-ahead we should proceed with caution and build up slowly.** Older muscles tear easily, joints are likely to be less flexible, ligaments less tolerant than they once were. Take advice on your medical readiness and do not overdo it!

The need is not for over exertion or the level of exercise that makes you tired, sweaty, out of breath, or in pain. *If you have taken medical advice*, are judged fit enough, and enjoy them, then senior level team games may be for you. The rest of us should aim rather for 'active living':

- Moderate activity (the kind that makes us warm and makes us breathe a bit more deeply – the equivalent of brisk walking) with which we are comfortable

- Activity which *invigorates* rather than tires us (this could include gardening, mowing the lawn, playing with children or grandchildren, climbing the stairs, housework, gentle dancing, swimming or cycling)

- 30 minutes a day, or most days (not necessarily all in one go – 3 x 10 minutes in the day can ease us in to it).

See www.healthyliving.gov.uk

Here are some tips which may be useful, if you have been medically advised to take up exercise.

- Warm up gradually before any exercise to prepare the body for increased activity. Gentle stretching exercises for the different areas of the body will protect against strains and pulled muscles.

- Aim for moderate exercise (say 30 minutes brisk walking) 4–5 days a week.

- Brisk walking means walking as if you are late for an appointment and you are slightly out of breath. You should be able to walk and talk at the same time; if you can't talk you are probably overdoing it!

- Aerobic exercise, which raises our heart and lung rate, is very important and valuable. If you are new to it, take medical advice first, and if given the go-ahead you can try brisk walking, biking, or swimming.

- The best fitness regimes include aerobic exercises, flexibility exercises, and strengthening exercises. (www.nhs.uk/livewell/fitness)

- A regularly active life, gardening, walking, energetic housework, dancing, using stairs not lifts, carrying shopping etc, can be as valuable as an exercise programme.

- Exercise with others, preferably with good-fun friends; the social element can help the motivation and the enjoyment.

- Listening to music while exercising can be a very pleasant distraction.

- Vary your activity programme. Changing activities, varying venues and routes, trying something new, can revive energy and interest.

- Work out the best time of day for your body. Some people are best in the morning, some in the evening and some all points in between.

- Eating healthily and always keeping your body hydrated will be the essential basis for regular physical activity.

- Wear appropriate clothes for exercise, they really help. They will increase your comfort and can reduce injury, especially footwear suited to your activity.

- Check your pulse frequently during exercise to make sure you are not overdoing it.

- Stop exercising immediately if you experience severe shortage of breath, coughing, pain or chest discomfort, dizziness, nausea, or any unusual symptoms, and consult your doctor.

- Fairly obviously – don't exercise in extremes of temperature, with a full stomach or when you are unwell.

- Choose activities you enjoy, because if you don't, your enthusiasm will soon wane.

- Cool down slowly; 5–10 minutes of gentle movement and stretching exercises to round off the greater exertions will help the body to ease itself back to normal.

A very valuable resource on exercise is 'Exercise – a program you can live with', a special health report by the Harvard Medical School, available on www.health.harvard.edu/special_health_reports/ Exercise.htm.

my work options

my finances

my relationships

my learning

my health and wellbeing

my leisure

my spirituality

my work options
my finances
my relationships
my learning
my health and wellbeing
my leisure
my spirituality

Life enhancers

Not everybody would agree that it is necessarily attractive to live longer if life is a drag, so be alert to factors that others say can make life even more rewarding at 50+. Could any of the following options enhance the second half of your life?

Life enhancer 1: sex and the older person

The poet Phillip Larkin famously stated that sex started in 1963. That was the way it seemed to him, but unfortunately for him he is not alive to see that, these days, a healthy sex life is not just for the younger person.

- Older people who have regular sex have better physical and mental health than those who don't.

- 'Self-esteem is better among older people who have sex; emotional wellbeing is greater and a feeling of togetherness exists which can be absent in others.' Dr Merryn Gott, the author of an article on the wellbeing of the over 50s, was reported in *The Observer*. The research was into married couples with an average age of 67 and most of the participants felt that 'sexual relationships made a valuable contribution to the quality of life' and considered it 'important that sexual needs are fulfilled'.

- The over 70s did report some reduction in sexual activity. One 74-year-old man reported 'we are all a bit craggy and you've all got something that's wrong physically – aches, pains, rheumatism', but a 74-year-old woman reported 'the older you get the more it just comes down to enjoying yourself. Without strings attached, it's back down to "as and when you want". When you have taken away procreation, sex is just enjoyment.'

- Other benefits of regular sexual activity were identified as 'a feeling of togetherness', 'sharing intimacy' and 'easing tension in a relationship'.

- There are challenges to overcome. One respondent reported 'the only thing that sometimes does put me off is that children never really grow up and leave home' and 'they and the grandchildren come and stay and that does interfere with my sex life. But at the end of the day we are all sexual beings – right up until rigor mortis sets in.' (!)

- Another problem, as longer and healthier lives are encouraging more casual and unprotected sex amongst older people: there have been dramatic increases in sexually transmitted diseases in the age group.

- In 2001, it was reported that HIV cases in the USA were rising among the over 50s at twice the rate found in younger people. In Britain, in 2007, while rates of gonorrhea and syphilis generally had risen by 55% in the previous five years, among the over 65s they had risen by 300%.

- An American study of people aged between 80 and 102, found that 83% of men and 30% of women indulged in intimacies other than intercourse.

- Some of the reduction in sex drive in older people can be down to the side-effects of medication being taken for other conditions such as blood pressure.

- Additionally there are new drugs that can assist in maintaining sexual drive. This is most definitely a subject it could be well worth discussing with your GP.

If you would like more information or advice on sex in the second half of your life you could search the internet using phrases such as 'sex and older people' or 'sex and ageing'. A website which is very helpful on this topic, as on others, is **www.helptheaged.org.uk**.

Life enhancer 2: stay mentally sharp

As we age, our ability to process information in our brain slows down – but not dramatically. Additionally, some of the medications associated with the second half of our lives can affect concentration and memory. We can compensate for that. We should be reassured that many of the great minds in history (and certainly many of the wisest people) have been in the 50+ age group. We can look after our minds while we are looking after our bodies.

'If we don't use it, we lose it!'

The brain and the mind have the best chance of thriving and prospering if we keep them active. A study of 19,000 women aged 70–81, published in the *Journal of the American Medical Association*, indicated that those who engaged in regular physical activity scored higher on a range of mental tests than those who were sedentary. Brain cells need oxygen, just like every other cell in our body. So, a good healthy diet and an active life are the basic essentials, but beyond that there are other ways for us to keep our brains functioning.

- Keep mentally active to avoid memory loss. Crossword puzzles, Sudoku, mentally challenging games, stimulating discussions, learning new skills, getting involved in further education (it is very common now for people in their 70s to take on further studies, even first and second degrees), learn and play a musical instrument, read widely, learn the computer, learn how to use mobile phones, cameras, DVD players, iPods!

- Have an active social life, meet people, take an interest in them, and get involved in your local community or church.

- Join walking groups, dance classes, debating societies, political parties, political movements, pressure groups, women's groups, men's clubs, sports clubs…

- Go to art classes, listen to discussions or comedy on the radio, take on new challenges, go to new places, watch good plays and films, do voluntary work that stretches you.

- Teach your grandchildren things as they grow, play games with them, read stories to them, tell them jokes.

- Don't marginalise yourself or let yourself be marginalised; stay involved in a range of activities.

- Have a purpose, an aim a goal for each day, each week, each month.

- Plan an agenda for each day.

- Travel if you can, it can actually broaden the mind!

Authors of *Teach Yourself Training Your Brain*, Terry Horne and Simon Wootton urge us not to accept that our brain power is genetically determined and fixed for life. They suggest that most of us only ever use up to 4% of our brain cells. They claim we can continue to increase our brain's health and mental capacity by how we live and work. They maintain that diet, environment and lifestyle will impact on our brain power. They recommend laughter, friends with shared interests, avoiding negative people and the pursuit of BLISS: Body-based pleasure; Laughter; Involvement; Satisfaction; and Sex. The claim is that all of these promote physical responses in us that benefit the health and wellbeing of our brains.

So, how do you plan to enhance your mental capacity and agility?

Resources

Search the internet with phrases such as: 'keeping minds active post 50', 'improving memory', 'learning at 50+', and see what might be possible.

Set yourself some targets in your locality to find out what's available in adult education that might be for you.

Look at learndirect offerings in eLearning.

Life enhancer 3: have fun

One suggestion, unproven, is that the average child laughs up to 300 times a day whilst the average adult laughs fewer than 20 times a day. The most miserable people apparently may raise a chuckle fewer than six times a day. Research-based or not, it is probably true that none of us laughs enough.

> *'There ain't much fun in medicine, but there is a heck of a lot of medicine in fun.'*
>
> *Josh Billings*

> *'The art of medicine consists of keeping the patient amused while nature heals the disease.'*
>
> *Voltaire*

> *'The simple truth is that happy people generally don't get sick.'*
>
> *Bernie Siegel M.D.*

The link between laughter and health is attracting attention in the medical world. At one stage, the suggestion was that 85% of all illnesses could be cured by the body's own healing system. Whether this is still the case or not, maintaining a happy and positive outlook on life is doubtless a very good way to support our wellbeing, Love, joy, caring, laughing are always going to be better for us than hating, nagging, moaning and groaning.

Laughter, it is thought, can:

- Build relationships – we warm to people who make us laugh and who laugh with us, and laughter bonds us to each other. We laugh 30 times more in company than we ever do alone.

- Be less a part of everyday life as we get older or become more senior at work.

- Reduce stress and strengthen the body's immune system.

- Exercise your heart: it raises the heartbeat and has been called 'internal jogging'. People with heart disease are 40% less likely to laugh in a variety of situations than people of the same age without heart disease.

- Help us deal with conflicts and crises, relax muscles and reduce tension.

- Indicate self-esteem; a lack of a sense of humour has been linked to low self-esteem.

my work options
my finances
my relationships
my learning
my health and wellbeing
my leisure
my spirituality

It is important of course to recognise that there is 'good' humour and 'bad' humour. Healthy humour is where we laugh together, laugh at ourselves or our situations – it brings us together with others. 'Bad' humour is when it is at other people's expense, when it hurts and distances people from us. That type is not likely to be therapeutic! So, laughter and fun are undoubtedly significant contributors to good health, especially as we age. So where do we find what we need? Why not:

- Decide each day to look at the funny side of life and look for laughs in everyday situations

- Spend time with funny friends or with children who can find fun in things much of the time

- Watch or listen to funny programmes

- Go to comedy films or shows. Comedy TV programmes usually have free tickets available for their recording sessions

- Look for cartoons and jokes in the daily papers – remember a joke a day and tell it to others

- Read humorous books

- Watch and listen to comedians, go to comedy clubs

- Don't spend too much time, if any, with grouches or pessimists

- Avoid news bulletins that focus on life tragedies and disasters that we can do little about

- Do a fun review at intervals – ask yourself am I getting enough?

On a scale of 1 to 10 (1 is 'little' – 10 is 'loads') how much fun and laughter is built into your life and work at present?

_____

Whatever your score is it probably could be higher. So what are you going to do about it?

I will:

_____

_____

_____

_____

_____

_____

_____

Resources

Try internet searches on:
'health and humour', 'fun and health', 'laughter and health', 'therapy and 'laughter', 'jokes'.

Websites:
www.helpguide.org
www.holisticonline.com/Humor_Therapy/humor_therapy.htm
www.psychologytoday.com

Books:
Laughter: a Scientific Investigation, Robert R Provine, (Penguin, 2001)
Health, Healing and the Amuse System, Paul E McGhee, (Kendal Hunt Pub. Co., 1996)

Life enhancer 4: cultivate gratitude!

'Gratitude is not only the greatest of all the virtues, but the parent of all the others.'

Cicero 106–43BC

Twenty-first century psychological research is suggesting that Cicero was on to something. If we define gratitude as when somebody experiences 'good fortune' and then expresses 'thanks or appreciation' in some way, then various research projects have indicated the following:

- 67% of people report that they experience gratitude 'all of the time' and 60% said that the experience made them feel 'very happy'.

- Many people have experienced enhanced feelings of gratitude since the 9/11 terrorist attack.

- Gratitude is a type of 'social cement' – it draws people together and invites reciprocation in terms of warmth and helpfulness.

- Gratitude is a characteristic of personality. Some people feel much more gratitude than others, feel it and express it more frequently and intensely, and feel it about a wider range of people and events.

- Gratitude is a key factor in an individual's experience of life-satisfaction and happiness.

- Increasing an individual's level of gratitude can increase their level of general wellbeing.

- Grateful people have closer social relationships and stronger support.

- Links between gratitude, sound mental health, hope and happiness are indicated and are being explored.

- There can be a virtuous cycle of increased gratitude leading to increased personal success leading to increased gratitude and so on.

(Based upon, Alex Wood, Stephen Joseph and Alex Linley (2007) 'Gratitude – parent of all virtues', *The Psychologist*, Vol. 20 No 1, January 2007.)

my work options

my finances

my relationships

my learning

my health and wellbeing

my leisure

my spirituality

> *'Gratitude is made from two words: great and attitude. If you have a great attitude, you have gratitude.'*
>
> *David Leonhardt*

Activity 5.3

Grateful for what?

Part 1

How much is gratitude part of your personality style?

■ What have you felt grateful for today?

_____

_____

_____

■ This week?

_____

_____

_____

■ How frequently did you express or convey that gratitude in some way? What are your reflections on that?

_____

_____

_____

Part 2

Here are some ways in which some people have built more gratitude into their lives (overleaf). Can you see yourself trying any of these? Tick the ones that you identify with.

my work options

my finances

my relationships

my learning

my health and wellbeing

my leisure

my spirituality

Building gratitude into our life – how some people do it	Could work for me?
I take exercise in the open air every day and notice nature – the trees, the birds, the clouds, the light, the wind, the rain – and am thankful I am alive and can still exercise.	
I ask myself at least three times a day 'What are the things I should be grateful for today?' and make sure I find something new each day.	
At work I try to look at things, events and people, positively, looking for things that go well or are helpful and I tell people what I appreciate.	
It's a cliché to 'count your blessings' but it actually is a piece of wisdom. I have been told so many times, when I am disappointed, to be grateful for what I've got and I find it works. It changes the focus.	
Making sure I look for some positives in any situation – for me the glass is always half full, never half empty.	
I keep a 'gratitude diary', noting down last thing before going to bed those things I am grateful for in the day just gone.	
I kind of 'meditate' on occasions about my life and my situation and recognise the things I am lucky to have or to be.	
I am grateful for the friends who bring me support, fun, relaxation and companionship and rejoice every time we are together.	
We have 'positive team' days at work, when we all have to notice the good things that people do to help each other and tell people what is good about working in our team.	
Write down the things that you see as the 'blessings' or 'riches', in your life and ask yourself, do you take these for granted?	
How do you build gratitude into your day? Write in what works for you.	

'The best kind of giving is thanksgiving!'

G K Chesterton

[end activity]

Activity 5.4

Gratitude checklist

Here is a list of things which people have indicated they are grateful for. How many of these are things that would be on your list? Tick the ones that you identify with.

- Each new morning, waking up and being able to get up ☐
- Having a job to go to when not everybody has ☐
- My health and our health services ☐
- Living in a country where we have food and security ☐
- Family and the support that brings ☐
- Friends and the good times we share ☐
- Music and my hearing that lets me enjoy it! ☐
- A 'good book' that gives me days of enjoyment ☐
- A great film or show that 'lifts me' ☐
- Travel, the ability to see places my parents only heard about ☐
- Children and especially grandchildren for the blessings, and challenges, they bring ☐
- Reaching each birthday 'landmark' ☐
- New technology which expands my world and my knowledge ☐
- Being in love and being loved ☐
- My partner ☐
- Being unique, realising I am a 'one-off' and therefore special and different ☐
- Sport and the many pleasures it brings to play and to watch ☐
- Other people who have different talents and skills from me and who are interesting to work with and learn from ☐
- Education and learning which has opened minds and horizons and is endless ☐
- My garden, full of life and colour and a source of so much interest and pleasure ☐.
- My house, a place of comfort and really nice to come home to ☐
- Having good food and wine to share with friends ☐
- The emergency services, there in our crises ☐
- Nature, the earth, the sea, the sky always there and always changing ☐
- The fact that I can walk, talk, move, hear, see, think ☐
- My pets, always loyal and comforting ☐
- Just having enough of everything when half of the world doesn't ☐
- Fun, when you can laugh loud and long ☐
- The BBC, the best in the world ☐

my work options

my finances

my relationships

my learning

my health and wellbeing

my leisure

my spirituality

my work options

my finances

my relationships

my learning

my health and wellbeing

my leisure

my spirituality

- Recovering from an illness ☐
- Seeing a loved one get better ☐
- Having things to celebrate, family achievements, birthdays, Christmas, people coming to stay ☐
- The countryside and night skies ☐
- The seasons, each one special, each one different ☐
- My allotment, an oasis of peace and quiet, close to nature, getting my hands in the soil, and good fresh vegetables on the table ☐

This list of course is endless because each of us in our unique life has many things to appreciate and be grateful for, even if sometimes we are more conscious of our problems. What additionally would you want to add to the list of things you are especially grateful for?

_____

_____

_____

_____

[end activity]

Some people have found gratitude is such a powerful element in making their life a positive experience that they build it into their daily lives.

My gratitude diary

Keeping a 'gratitude diary' is a way of requiring our thoughts to turn each day to gratitude and has been used successfully by people needing to move on from negative times in their lives – as well as by those who just want to live more positively.

– It can simply be a special diary or note book to which you turn daily or weekly, to write in the date and the time and anything you wish to record that you are grateful for at that time.

– You can use a set methodology such as beginning what you write with 'today I am grateful for…' and listing the thoughts that occur to you.

– The practice usually requires a quiet time and place to promote reflection.

– You can, if it helps, have a format for the reflection by having categories to focus on e.g. 'For myself, I am grateful that… ', 'As a woman (or man), I am grateful for…', 'For my family, I am grateful that… ', 'In my work, I am grateful that…', 'In my life, I am grateful that…', 'For my friends, I am grateful that…', 'In the news, I am grateful that…' etc.

– If you have the skills and the time, these journals could become works of art with thoughts illustrated and enhanced by sketches, by colours, by poems etc.

(Based upon the work of Dr Robert Emmons and Dr Michael McCullough **http://psychology.ucdavis. edu/labs/emmons**.)

There are two key features in expanding the benefits that gratitude can bring:

- Consciously thinking about, looking for and reflecting on gratitude and its place in your daily life with all its dimensions

- Expressing, conveying, communicating gratitude genuinely to others, to enhance their experience of it and create the reciprocation it produces.

Gratitude is infectious and contagious. It builds on people's strengths and generosity. It creates wellbeing and even happiness. It is hugely valuable and important.

'Here is a one-sentence formula for becoming a grateful person; Think gratefully, Speak gratefully, Act gratefully.'

Rabbi Zelig Plishkin

144

Life enhancer 5: get the basics right – ageing healthily

Whatever you have taken from this section, it would be good to finish by reminding ourselves of the basic messages of living healthily so we can make the most of our life and career plans for the second half of our lives. All the research into the area is fascinating, but the basic messages seem to be consistent and universal. They are that if we want the best chance of living a long, fruitful and happy life, we should:

- Not smoke
- Avoid alcohol abuse
- Enjoy good, stable relationships
- Do physical and mental exercise
- Eat healthily and maintain a healthy weight
- Avoid, or cope well with, stressful situations
- Meditate, pray, relax; do things that restore us
- Contribute to a cause, something we care about
- Continue learning
- Laugh more
- Enjoy an active sex life
- Be involved in social and productive activities
- Be positive and look for the good things in life
- Show gratitude
- Have regular medical checks
- Sleep well to restore body and mind.

Reflecting on your life at the moment:

■ how many of the above are part of your life now?

_____
_____
_____
_____
_____

■ which might you wish to make some plans to work on?

_____
_____
_____
_____
_____

Finding out more

There is a very comprehensive health and lifestyle check on **www.realage.com**, which also produces lifestyle recommendations based on your score. It is American, so a few questions may be more difficult to answer because of differences in medical terminology.

Web resources

www.thirdage.com/health
www.helpguide.org
www.holisticonline.com/Humor_Therapy/humor_
  therapy.htm
www.psychologytoday.com
www.eatwell.gov.uk
www.nutrition.org.uk
www.bupa.co.uk
www.diabetes.co.uk
www.health.harvard.edu
www.helptheaged.org.uk
taen@helptheaged.org.uk
www.ageconcern.org.uk
www.realage.com
www.workingforhealth.gov.uk
sleepresearch@lboro.ac.uk
www.fiftyforward.co.uk

A former BBC news presenter was once ridiculed for suggesting that there should be 'good news' programmes. Research is now suggesting that he might have been correct, in that our constant diet of bad news stories really can invite depression. A free US website, **www.gimundo.com**, which was set up to counter this, is worth subscribing to; it only communicates good news stories.

Summary

You have had the opportunity to reflect on and find out more about:

- Healthy living through diet and exercise
- The link between work and health
- Life enhancers, which can add to the quality of our lives.

Action plans

On the basis of your reflections on your current health and wellbeing, and the information you have surveyed in this section, write in what you would like more of, less of and what you would like to keep the same in your life right now. Reflect on your diet, exercise, work and life enhancers and plan any changes you would like to make.

my work options
my finances
my relationships
my learning
my health and wellbeing
my leisure
my spirituality

my work options

my finances

my relationships

my learning

my health and wellbeing

my leisure

my spirituality

MORE OF...	LESS OF...	KEEP THE SAME

Choose three that you would like to start working on right now:

1. _____

2. _____

3. _____

'Job satisfaction and self-worth are more important than salary alone. Money helps, but it doesn't buy health, happiness or a clear conscience.'

Jim, in his 60s

my leisure

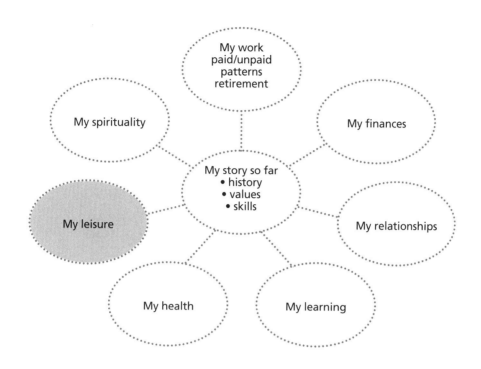

Introduction

There are unprecedented leisure options for the 50+ age group, many of whom who are 'time and money rich', having spent their last three decades committed to career-building and/or family-raising. Having reached 50+, some of us may need to re-learn how to 'play' or even 'adventure'. This section will invite exploration of, and answers to, questions such as:

- What leisure time pursuits might fit with your interests?

- What do you gain from your leisure time?

- Are there other things you might like to explore in your leisure time?

An HSBC *'Future of Retirement'* report in 2007 found that retirees in the baby boomer generation (people aged between 52 and 60), have achieved a form of perfect work–life balance that Generation X (people in their 30s and 40s) strive for, but may never afford.

> *'I don't know if it's because time goes quicker when you are older but I seem to have less time for leisure than when I was younger. Travel has become my special interest. My wife and I take two holidays abroad each year and go to far-flung places like Nepal, China, Thailand.'*
>
> Chris Read, in his 60s.

> *'I do degrees the way other people do long-distance walks!'*
>
> Mary, in her 70s

my work options

my finances

my relationships

my learning

my health and wellbeing

my leisure

my spirituality

my work options

my finances

my relationships

my learning

my health and wellbeing

my leisure

my spirituality

Do you know?

- Those over 50 now take 35% of all trips abroad; new research from the Foreign & Commonwealth Office (FCO, 2008) reveals that nearly 70% of over 50s say they are more adventurous with their trips now than they used to be ten years ago. Almost a fifth of those questioned have taken part in adventure activities, such as bungee jumping or abseiling, with 25% looking to swim with dolphins. With that in mind, the FCO is advising the over 50s to start making better preparations for their adventurous travels.

- The older generation is taking full advantage of cheap airfares; the over 50s take an average of eight or nine holidays each year, compared with just one or two in 1957.

- The average spend on holidays has risen from £128 to £845, adjusted for inflation. The number of trips taken beyond Europe and North America by people aged between 55 and 64 has doubled to 1.23 million annually, over the last ten years. Over 65s are more cautious, but they have doubled their visits to continental Europe over the same period, to 4.8 million. Pensioners are now worth £3.1 billion annually to the travel industry, three times the amount they spent in 1995.

- A report, commissioned by intune, a financial services subsidiary of Help the Aged, shows the over 50s taking personal fitness just as seriously as younger generations did 50 years ago. They take part in the same amount of sport as 25-year-olds did in 1957, at an hour a week. When time spent on hobbies is added on, they spend almost three hours a week more on all leisure activities than their counterparts 50 years ago.

- 43% of over 50s who use the internet regularly buy and sell via eBay.

- Britain's consumer bug has also bitten the older generation, who are energetic shoppers. They spend twice as much time shopping as their counterparts in the 1950s. Those over retirement age actually spend more time shopping than those aged between 16 and 24 today, at an average of three hours 40 minutes a week compared with one hour 48 minutes.

- But to accommodate all the holidaying, shopping and time on the golf course, housework has taken a hit. The over 50s spent six hours 39 minutes a week cleaning their home in 1957. Today's older generation makes do with three hours and five minutes.

- It is clear that people of 50+ in the 'noughties' seem more inclined to spend their time socialising with friends or family, travelling or indulging in hobbies than they are to clean and tidy or do household repairs. That is not to say that they do not do these things – they just do them for comparatively less time than other activities.

- This means that, in comparison to those aged 45 in 1961, those currently aged 45–64 spend on average 189 hours per year less cleaning and tidying; the over 65s spend 183 hours less on this activity. This is almost 12 waking days (of 16 hours) fewer on cleaning and tidying: the equivalent of a holiday abroad, or perhaps two or three short breaks.

- Another way to see this is that, over the course of a post-retirement life stage (average 18.5 years), a twenty-first century older person will spend seven and a half months engaged in activities that in the past would have been spent in domestic drudgery.

- Some reasons for this may be that developments in technology make housework considerably less time-intensive; there has also been a significant increase in out-sourcing of domestic work during the period in question.

- "Anyone for tennis?" – the over 50s are taking part in the same amount of sport as done by those aged between 16 and 44 years, 50 years ago; there has been a fourfold increase in time spent on sport and exercise by over 50s in the past 50 years.

- Leisure lovers: over 65s today currently spend almost three hours a week more than their counterparts 50 years ago, engaging in hobbies and sports.

- People aged 65–74 have the highest levels of volunteering of all older people.

- The fact that older generations are keeping in touch with technology is not something that has gone unnoticed. Home multimedia use, which includes TV, radio, music and internet, has increased exponentially since 1961 and one effect of this has been that those aged 45–54 spend a full day longer, per week, on home multimedia than they did in 1961. In 2006, of those who use the internet (56% of 45–64s and 20% of the over 65s), the over 65s spent two and a half hours per week online and 45–64s spent almost five hours.

my work options

my finances

my relationships

my learning

my health and wellbeing

my leisure

my spirituality

Activity 6.1

Which leisure interests to pursue?

Look at your interest scores, if you have already done them. If not go to 'My story so far…' and complete Activity 7.

What are your main areas of interest? Are they: ARTISTIC, ENTERPRISING, SOCIAL, PRACTICAL, FINDING OUT or ROUTINE?

Below is a list of examples of leisure interests that fit for each of these main interest areas. These lists suggest activities that might more closely match your interests. It does not imply that you will have the necessary skills, only the motivation to try out these leisure activities.

Tick those which interest you, or about which you would like to find out more.

PRACTICAL INTERESTS – possible leisure links

Repairing or mending things
Bike or horse riding
Walking, hiking, running
Camping, caravanning
Playing football, cricket, hockey, netball
Making things, such as models or dressmaking, using patterns or instruction kits
Cooking
Car or bike racing
Gardening, allotments
Do-it-yourself
Mountain climbing
Ice skating, roller skating
Aerobic dancing, fitness classes
Skiing
Skin diving/scuba diving
Bicycling alone to exercise
Working out in a gym
Jogging alone
Swimming
Archery
Training animals
Hang gliding, sky diving
Carpentry
Candle making
Wine making
Sewing
Bee keeping
Restoring cars, furniture, houses

NB – Please note that those who have not engaged very much in an active life post 50 should definitely take medical advice before launching yourself on any activity above requiring physical exertion. If given the go-ahead, build up your fitness level over time!

FINDING OUT INTERESTS – possible leisure links

Developing and processing photos
Reading books and magazines on scientific or technical subjects
Observing, collecting, identifying such things as birds, animals, plants, fossils, shells, rocks etc.
Visiting museums, scientific or technical displays
Watching and listening to documentaries or in-depth reports on TV, radio or internet
Playing chess, draughts, bridge, scrabble, mastermind, or other games of skill and mental agility
Computer programming
Research involving the internet
Genealogy
Self-development
Alternative therapies
Meditation
Attending lectures
Various adult education courses

SOCIAL INTERESTS – possible leisure links

Visiting and working with the handicapped, older people, etc.
Taking part in guides, scouts, youth groups, church and religious groups
Planning and giving parties
Running or walking with others
Raising funds for charities
Working with young children in play groups, Sunday schools, cubs, brownies, etc.
Activities with family
Playing games or sport with friends or family
Spending social time with friends or work colleagues at pubs, dinner parties, restaurants
Massage or martial arts (or possibly both though not at once!)

Joining clubs or activities primarily for the social functions

Using the computer for social contacts and networking, e.g. my space, instant messenger, bebo, Facebook, etc.

Travelling, with friends or a group

Playing games, where winning is not the most important thing

Playing computer games which need other players

Belonging to virtual communities such as Second Life

Shopping with friends

ARTISTIC INTERESTS – possible leisure links

Learning or playing a musical instrument or singing

Writing short stories or poetry

Sketching, drawing or painting

Taking part in plays or musicals

Designing websites or new computer games

Craft work e.g. pottery, weaving, knitting, jewellery making, macramé

Visiting art galleries, exhibitions, cinema, plays or concerts

Flower arranging

Yoga

Photography

Gem polishing

Dancing – ballroom, salsa, etc.

Interior decorating

Restoring antiques

Sculpting

Visiting National Trust or similar properties or gardens

Singing in a choir

ENTERPRISING INTERESTS – possible leisure links

Playing Monopoly, backgammon, poker or games of chance

Doing small jobs, such as gardening or car cleaning or repairs for a fee

Taking part in debates or making speeches

Starting a debating group

Following politics in the newspaper, or on radio, TV or internet

Serving on a committee

Earning money by selling things

Car boot sales

Games where winning is important

Soccer, rugby, snooker, darts, cards, bicycle and motor racing (if winning is not important, the interest will be social)

Making homebrew beer or wine to save money

Entering craft work in competitions

Promoting charities or fund raising

ROUTINE INTERESTS – possible leisure links

Using calculators or computers for record keeping

Keeping detailed accounts or a careful diary

Tidying up sheds, cupboards, drawers, etc.

Keeping times and recording results at sporting events

Collecting and cataloguing coins, stamps, photo albums scrap books

Calligraphy

Designing timetables for social events

[end activity]

Now that you have spent some time thinking of all of your possible areas of interest, it's time to start analysing some of them in more detail

My favourite leisure activities

From the list of possible leisure activities in the previous activity, now pick your ten favourite ones.

Think carefully about them, and then list the top 10 in the table below, putting your favourite at number 1. Include any that you would like to try but have not yet got around to doing.

Each of the columns asks you a question about that activity. Write in the letter or symbol suggested to build up a picture of how you are using your leisure time or ideally would like to spend it.

My top leisure activities (please list them here)	Carried out alone (A) or with people (P)?	Tick or add a £ symbol if it costs £10 or more	Does it involve risk? Indicate physical (P), intellectual (I), or emotional (E)	Energetic (E) or non-energetic (NE)?	Do you do this often (O), sometimes (S) or rarely (R)?	Date when you last did it
1						
2						
3						
4						
5						
6						
7						
8						
9						
10						

[end activity]

From working with people using these exercises we found one person discovered that he needed a balance between 'doing things with others' and 'doing things alone'; at present he was not spending enough time doing things alone. Another person was not surprised to find a high level of physical risk in her activities, but realised she was not making enough time for them. One person found that he was doing hardly any of the things that he really enjoyed.

One wife realised that her favourite activities cost her almost nothing, which pleased her, and her husband found three activities from the previous exercise that he had never thought of doing but now had included in his list.

Interestingly, another person, a very successful store manager (ENTERPRISING) realised that he did not want leisure pursuits that were driven by that interest. Instead, and as a complete contrast, he liked to experiment with digital photography (ARTISTIC).

What do your entries say about your leisure life?

Finding out more

Ask your friends if any of them engage in any leisure activities not included in the lists.

Web resources

- http://www.laterlife.com/online-store-gifts-presents-christmas/travel-offers-holiday-offers.htm

- If you want to spend more time exploring your, and your family's, past history you could consult www.cyndislist.com or www.ancestry.co.uk to get you started.

- If you wanted to record your own life story you can try www.lifediary.com or www.lifelinespress.co.uk.

- If you want to volunteer abroad, VSO are now offering short-term positions lasting from two weeks to six months for people up to 75 (www.vso.org.uk).

- For new leisure possibilities explore www.silversurfers.net and www.over50s-silversurfers.co.uk.

- If you want to see what you can create on the web, look at www.silversurfers.net/silversurfers-sitesof.html.

- Try an internet search for 'leisure for the over 50s'.

- For more information please visit www.fiftyforward.co.uk

Summary

You have looked at leisure interests that you might pursue and rank ordered your favourites.

my work options
my finances
my relationships
my learning
my health and wellbeing
my leisure
my spirituality

Action plans

On the basis of your reflections on your current leisure profile, and the alternatives you have surveyed in this section, write in what you would like more of, less of and what you would like to keep the same in your leisure life right now.

MORE OF...	LESS OF...	KEEP THE SAME

Choose three that you would like to start exploring now:

1. _____

2. _____

3. _____

'Leisure? I have been playing since I was 22 and getting paid for it!'

Mike Pegg

my work options
my finances
my relationships
my learning
my health and wellbeing
my leisure
my spirituality

Notes

my spirituality

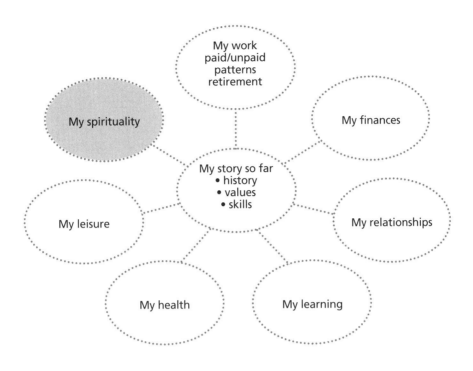

'Spirituality is being concerned with things of the spirit – the big questions of meaning, metaphysics, existence. Being spiritual is thinking about, wondering about and exploring the deepest aspects of reality, values, morals and meanings.'

Amara Rose www.helpguide.org

Introduction

The inclusion of this topic in a process of career and life planning may seem surprising but, for many, as we age and begin to realise we are indeed in 'the second half' of our lives, the spiritual element of life can take on a new focus. At some point, as we age, we become curious about 'how long have we got left and how do we want to spend that time?'.

In our prime, confidence and certainty had probably abounded. We were 'the' generation the world had been waiting for; we were the key to the future; we would find the answers; just move the 'wrinklies' aside. And now, as we progress into that second half, we may be realising that:

- We are not immortal

- Our physical and mental conditions and capacities are not all they once were

- Our friends are perhaps not as robust as they once were

- Our children, if we had any, have fled the nest and are now the confident futurists we once were

- Our parents, if still around, are becoming more fragile, less mobile and more in need of our care

- Some of our old certainties have perhaps been replaced by some doubts and questions.

These factors can cause us to begin to reflect again (or perhaps for the first time) on 'the bigger questions' of life, such as:

- What is life all about?

- Why are we here?

- How should we approach the rest of our life?

- What are success and happiness now?

- What is important at our age and stage?

- How should we spend the time and resource we seem to have in greater abundance than in our earlier life?

- What contribution, if any, should we make to our offspring, our parents, our wider community?

- What kind of world should we seek to bequeath to our children, grandchildren and future generations?

- What will our legacy be?

- What do we want from the time we have left?

If we have a strictly material and scientific view of a human being, then the answers may be uncomplicated. Maybe we really are just a collection of DNA, with a limited lifespan, with a capacity to breed and perpetuate the species, do what the genes require and what our appetites and needs demand, for as long as we can keep going – and then pass away as peacefully and painlessly as possible.

For other people, that strictly physical view of the human does not feel or sound quite right; it is not totally aligned with their experience of life. In being born, in loving others, in experiencing the highs and lows of life, in friendships, in teams, in achievements, in giving birth, in losing and burying, in the wonders, beauty and power of nature, in the rhythms of the seasons, in the vastness of the universe – in so many contexts we sense a dimension beyond the merely physical.

'The spiritual quest begins, for most people, as a search for meaning.'

Marilyn Ferguson

What is spirituality?

Spirituality is different to religion, though many people find their spiritual base in the major world religions. The *Oxford Dictionary of English* defines 'religion' as;

'the belief in and worship of a superhuman controlling power, especially a personal god or gods; a particular system of faith and worship.'

…and 'spirituality' as:

'relating to or affecting the human spirit or soul as opposed to material or physical things; having a relationship based on a profound level of mental or emotional communion.'

In a recent British survey, 39% of people said they would describe themselves as 'not religious', whereas only 12% said they would describe themselves as 'not spiritual'. As long ago as 2002, the number of books published on non-Christian spirituality surpassed the Christian portfolio.

While many in Britain and Europe are turning away from religion, for various reasons, many more are searching for 'spiritual meaning' in their lives. Religion, with its creeds and its dogmas and its different routes to God and everlasting life, has been seen by some as dividing the world and its peoples, in an age where we are becoming more conscious of living in one 'global village'. But that 'turning away' does not always bring the answers to many of the 'big questions' that have intrigued human beings over millennia.

Spirituality is being interpreted in different ways, as having to do with:

- The 'non-material', 'non-physical' part of ourselves or our world

- That which is 'at the heart of us', the very essence of us when ego is set aside; some would say 'our very soul and spirit' that makes us who we are

- Connecting with, and articulating, 'the beyond' in our lives

- A focus on 'creation, or nature, or a sense of order in the cosmos'

- The 'big questions' of life

- Addressing our 'smallness against the vastness of the

universe', leading to views on ourselves and others, on the world, on existence

- An emotional response to major life events such as birth, death, love, loss

- Reflections on events and experiences bringing feelings of significance, unity, acceptance, connection, serenity, joy, reconciliation, celebration, transcendence.[21]

('I wanted…) to find renewed meaning and purpose in my life. I no longer found working with organisations/management/committees energising. I felt the need of refreshment and renewal and wanted to find something that would meet my own needs. I felt the need to get closer to my own inner world.'

Mildred Neville, in her 80s

A level of spirituality can be experienced in the comradeship of people who share extreme challenges or adversity together, such as mineworkers, trawler crews, firefighters, mountaineers.

'We are not human beings having a spiritual experience. We are spiritual beings having a human experience.'

Pierre Teilhard de Chardin

Spiritual stimulus can come from religion, meditation, music, literature, poetry, friendship, conviviality. It can be triggered by awesome natural settings (landscapes and seascapes) or events, by night skies, dawns, changing seasons, sunsets, or vast silences. It has been encouraged by rituals and ceremonies, by the celebration of a New Year and the passing of the old, by shared community experiences. Some have found it in sporting or other bonding experiences (e.g. demonstrations in support of causes such as civil rights; the anti-war protests at Greenham Common, etc.). Some have detected a spiritual dimension in liberating political movements – examples of this could include the outlawing of slavery, the women's movement, the Black Consciousness Movement against apartheid in South Africa or the resistance of monks, students and the oppressed inspired by Aung San Suu Kyi to the brutal regime in Burma. Gandhi used the spiritual dimension of his Indian culture to inspire his campaign of non-violent resistance to British rule. Nelson Mandela's hugely mature philosophy of non-reprisal against the oppressive

21 Based on, and inspired by, *Religion in Exile*, Diarmuid O'Murchu, Gateway, 2000

white regime, after 25 years behind bars, spoke volumes to many of a spiritual vision for his country's future, as did 'the dream' of Martin Luther King of a future of freedom and equality for black Americans.

'Ethical existence is the highest manifestation of spirituality.'

Albert Schweitzer

Spirituality in this sense is to do with 'transcendence' and addresses our personal integrity, our relationships with others, the values that underpin how we live our lives. While religions can address the hope of an afterlife, spirituality can focus on 'horizontal transcendence', an engagement with 'otherness,' with our world and its wellbeing. It can address a sense of purpose, order and wholeness in the universe. This spirituality takes the longer view and suggests more than the temporality of everyday life. This is a spirituality which is about 'our world', addressing 'what are we here for?' It motivates us to work for what we care deeply about. Connecting values and purpose can be a spiritual force.

'Respect the flow of life…the positive energy in life…and try to be true to it…put positive things into the world…words, feelings, ideas…'

Mike Pegg, in his 60s

'There is no higher religion than human service. To work for the common good is the gentlest creed.'

Albert Einstein

Some would say:

- Our unique, individual 'stories' (our unique life histories) have a spiritual element – sharing them, and recognising and respecting achievements and uniqueness, can build relationships with a spiritual dimension

- We grow and prosper only through loving and being loved; such experiences give us 'an inkling' of a bigger potential experience

- The public expression of love after disasters such as 9/11, or the 2006 tsunami, are examples of love made visible on a vast scale

- Spirituality is apparent in statements such as the 'Universal Declaration of Human Rights', in the

157

Geneva Convention, in the opening statements of the American Constitution.

'The spiritual journey is individual, highly personal. It cannot be organised or regulated. It isn't true that everybody should follow one path. Listen to your own truth.'

Ram Dass

See what one of the respondents to our questionnaire has to say about ice cream being a source for him of a particular spiritual perspective:

'Two different experiences involving ice cream:

1) a friend, terminally ill with a brain tumour who I was taking out for the day. I asked him what he had eaten for lunch; the answer was five scoops of ice cream.

2) an orphan in Cape Town who was given by us his first ice cream.

The thing in common was the look of pleasure linked to the ice cream and the lesson for us to enjoy all experiences to the full, as though they were our last or our first. Never just pass through life.'

Ian Walker, in his 50s

Spirituality motivates us to work always for interdependence, for connectedness, for universalism, for sustainability, non-divisiveness, the good of humanity and 'creation'.

Life stages

In *Your Soul at Work*[22], authors Weiler and Schoonover draw on the work done by psychologists Erikson, Levinson and others into 'life stages'. This work suggests that, just as there are development stages in childhood, so also are there stages in adult life. Adulthood is not one permanent 'condition' but rather a series of periods, each having different features, emphases, priorities. For the over 50s, the suggestion in *Your Soul at Work* is that there are at least two further stages in life. The first of these occurs somewhere between our chronological ages of 50 to 65 (the stages are not tied definitively to chronological ages) and is called 'leaving a legacy'. This life stage, the authors suggest, is typified by:

- Being particularly productive after the uncertainties of the better-known 'mid-life crisis'

- The 'peaking' of our 'mature abilities' and the making of our 'greatest possible contributions to others and society'

- Our being 'less-driven, less ego-centred, less compelled to compete and impress'

- A focus on 'what really matters to us, on developing others, on community, on leaving some personal legacy that really makes things better for people (whether that is recognised or not), on accomplishing goals that our maturity and greater spirituality tell us have the most true meaning in the overall scheme of life'.

The next – and final – life stage, which can go on for many years after our mid-60s, they call 'spiritual denouement'. In this stage, they suggest, we:

- Are 'tying things up, completing the design of what we want to become, finalising our growth and assessing/fine-tuning the persons we have made of ourselves'

- 'Come to grips with the ultimate limitations of life, ourselves and mortality'

- Can 'look hopefully and unflinchingly at the ultimate meaning of our life and the life of others'

- Do what we can to 'pass on to others whatever wisdom we have gained'

- 'Accept others for what they are', see them 'growing like we are and accepting them as part of humankind's diversity'.

> **Do you know?**
>
> - Some architects recognise a spiritual dimension in buildings – they work to design places which 'inspire', encourage, foster, those who will live and work in them.
>
> *'When the spirit does not work with the hand there is no art.'*
>
> *Leonardo Da Vinci*
>
> - The workplace 2017 – in an article 'It's work, but not as we know it', Liz Hollis in *The Guardian* (September 2007) reports that 'futurist' Anne Lise Kjaer predicts that the workplace will have to

22 *Your Soul at Work*, Nicholas W Weiler, Cowley Publications USA, 2003

change radically over the next decade to attract the new generation of 'e-lancers'. There will need to be a 'home-from-home vibe', with giant communal desks, showers, 'chill-out' zones, and a 'pod' for power naps after virtual meetings across time zones – required to attract e-lancers in two days a week at times of their choice. Kjaer predicts 'Within a few years, the very phrase "going to work" will be meaningless. Work will be what we do, not a place we go to.'

She believes these social trends will drive the changes; smart technology; globalisation; the rise of the Asian economies; female empowerment ; and increasing spiritual and emotional awareness. She observes we are entering 'an emotional decade' in which 'ethics and spirituality will prevail in the workplace. People have discovered that money alone doesn't buy happiness and they will be looking elsewhere for meaning. She continues: 'To attract and retain the people they need, businesses will have to go beyond the salary package. They will need to 'empower workers and enhance their physical and mental wellbeing too. We will want work to be life enhancing and the companies we work for to be ethical. We will be looking for emotional connection and empowerment on all levels.'

- Some psychologists and brain experts now recognise that, rather than just the traditional view that we each have a single IQ, we have many types of intelligence, including emotional intelligence and spiritual intelligence. Maslow's hierarchy of needs that we discussed earlier ('Theme 1: My work options') is sometimes now depicted with spirituality at the peak of the pyramid.

  One version of Maslow's pyramid of needs has self-actualisation and spirituality as its highest levels of need. At the higher levels of motivation, we have moved beyond the more self-centred levels towards working for spiritual goals such as fulfilment, meaning, truth, goodness, transcendence, perfection, harmony, justice and so on.

- Links are being explored between physical and mental health and religion and spirituality. The suggestion is that a strong religious or spiritual life can assist in helping us cope with ageing, with physical and mental illness, with crises and bereavements. This is achieved by increasing our involvement in healthy living, increasing our social support and by injecting meaning into our lives.

- There is a growing interest in the links between spirituality and the work place. 'Each of us will spend more of our waking hours working, or preparing for work, or recovering from work, than we spend on any other activity in our whole life… At the end of each day the universe is different than it was at the beginning, and our work is one of the most important aspects of that change.'[23]

- If such a huge amount of time is invested in work, then the challenge must be to make it meaningful and motivating. Individuals and teams working for higher goals, seeking achievements that benefit others beyond themselves, are likely to achieve levels of commitment and self-actualisation that bring success and reputation to their organisation.

'Human systems are also patterns of dynamic energy… From this perspective it's no longer about 'me and you' but about 'us'. It's not separation; it's integration. It's not isolation; it's an understanding that we are all part of one great big interwoven system. These new ideas are critical to understanding how we can make shifts in organisational culture, collaboration and teamwork.'

Danah Zohar discussing her book SQ; Connecting with Our Spiritual Intelligence *as reported on* **www.pegasuscom.com**

- Research by HSBC established that different countries have different attitudes to old age and retirement. The British see it as a time for self-sufficiency, independence, flexibility and personal responsibility. Americans see it as a time for opportunity, new careers and spiritual fulfilment.

- The gifts that the over 50s can bring to society are the focus of the work of *The Network of Spiritual Progressives* (www.spiritualprogressives.org). Michael Lerner writes 'our point is also that many elders have a wealth of wisdom which they may not recognise or label as "spiritual", but which really is… the central idea of our approach is that we need a new Bottom Line in America which sees institutions, social practices or human beings as valuable, efficient, rational and productive, not only to the extent that they maximise money and power, but also to the extent that they maximise love and caring, kindness and generosity, ethical and ecological sensitivity, enhance our capacities to

23 *Your Soul at Work; How to live Your Values in the Workplace*, Bryan A Hiebert, Northstone Publishing Inc., 2005

my work options

my finances

my relationships

my learning

my health and wellbeing

my leisure

my spirituality

respond to others as embodiments of the sacred and to respond to the universe with awe and wonder. Our society can't figure out a way to use people to make profits, so they are no longer considered valuable. And this whole notion of what is valuable is what we challenge.'

- Dr Susan Stewart, Professor of Psychology at Sonoma State University, has explored what Carl Jung described as the 'treasure trove' of world myth – the stories that have been built up about classical heroes and heroines – and linked these to current work on ageing. World myth and a 'growing body of research' show that there are potential 'gifts of the second half of life'. These are, she suggests:

1. **increasing wisdom:** the ability to 'see' things more clearly, to have a deeper understanding, and to 'do the right thing'

2. **enhanced creativity:** in thought, in expression, and in lifestyle

3. **greater freedom from social norms:** the readiness to break conventions, to 'do one's own thing', to live one's own life despite disapproval

4. **emotional mastery:** being at ease with oneself and one's feelings, expressing feelings in non-harmful ways, having a balanced view whatever the circumstances, an enhanced capacity for healthy humour and a readiness to laugh at oneself

5. **increased tolerance:** having an acceptance of and compassion for others

6. **growing appreciation:** for 'the small, the slow, the subtle, and the simple'

7. **tolerance for paradox and uncertainty:** the 'return of awe and wonder and a deepening appreciation of the mystery of life'

8. **a capacity for transcendence and surrender:** moving beyond concerns for one's ego, personality and appearance; letting go of the need for control and becoming an 'instrument of life, willing to do what is needed for the greater good'.

She does point out that these 'gifts of the second half' are *possibilities*, not *guarantees*. They require both willingness and work!

- In March 2007, a Canadian Philosopher, Charles Taylor, aged 75, won the £800,000 Templeton Prize for Progress Toward Research or Discoveries about Spiritual Realities, for his work in linking a search for meaning to the recruitment of young people to terrorist groups. He warns 'There are certain kinds of hunger that people have, including a sense of meaning in life, that comprises the spiritual dimension… These terrorists are motivated by the need to be connected to a big cause. The only way they can be prevented from heading for terrorism is to have a better answer to the meaningfulness of life.'

'He who has a 'why' to live for can bear almost any 'how'

Nietzsche

'Some day, after we have mastered the winds, the waves, the tides and gravity, we shall harness the energies of love. Then, for the second time in the history of the world, humankind will have discovered fire.'

Pierre Teilhard de Chardin

my work options

my finances

my relationships

my learning

my health and wellbeing

my leisure

my spirituality

Activity 7.1

How spiritual am I?

Reflect on the following statements and how much they might – or might not – apply to you. Score them as follows:

2 – if they **very much** apply to you
1 – if they **somewhat** apply to you
0 – if they **do not** apply to you.

In general

■ I have a sense that there is more to life than the physical, material world that we experience everyday. ☐

■ I believe that my life has meaning, purpose and value beyond material gain or reward. ☐

■ People looking at the way I work and my lifestyle would guess I am motivated by things other than 'the material' things of life'. ☐

■ I can describe myself without reference to my job and have pride in that description. ☐

■ It is very important to me to have a reputation for:

  – honesty ☐

  – truth ☐

  – compassion ☐

  – generosity ☐

  – peacemaking ☐

  – patience ☐

  – integrity ☐

  – co-operation ☐

  – gratitude ☐

  – loyalty ☐

  – love ☐

  – friendship ☐

  – teamship ☐

  – empathy ☐

  – creating unity ☐

  and I work hard to build such a reputation. ☐

■ I frequently reflect on life and my part in it and wonder what I can do to make things better. ☐

■ I give time regularly to reflect and ponder on 'the bigger questions', reflecting on what is my purpose, meaning and contribution in life. ☐

■ People report having experienced spiritual moments in particular settings such as: being present at the birth of their child; at a great musical performance; in the presence of great works of art; in strikingly beautiful natural settings, landscapes, seascapes; in gardening and working with nature; in witnessing the force of nature in storms or earthquakes; in moments of great threat or fear or near-death situations; at a moment of outstanding achievement; in a loving relationship; at the loss of a loved one; etc.

I know what they mean, because I have had a similar experience. ☐

■ The source of my spirituality is in religious belief. ☐

At work

■ I believe *people* are much more than their work, their salary level and the status of their job. ☐

■ I believe *I* am more than my work, my salary level and the status of my job. ☐

■ I commit to high performance, believing we should each offer the best of our talents and gifts to the 'common good'. ☐

■ I genuinely rejoice in the achievements of others. ☐

■ I prize highly being a member of a team and sharing in collective performance. ☐

■ I make great effort in building positive relationships with colleagues, customers and even competitors. ☐

■ I make great efforts to make the workplace a happy and positive place. ☐

■ I am appreciative of the support and encouragement I get from others. ☐

■ I experience pride in creating products, services or results that benefit society. ☐

■ I enjoy working in a culture in which respect and compassion for people is very apparent. ☐

■ I actually do believe that people are the most important resource in an organisation. ☐

■ I am very committed to my continuing development, as I want to make the most of all my potential. ☐

■ I can see a spiritual dimension to the work I do. ☐

In the community and the world

■ I give time and effort in contributing to the betterment of my local community. ☐

■ I give my time and abilities to working for the disadvantaged. ☐

■ I am committed to and spend time on causes that benefit others without material return for me. ☐

■ I am conscious of the challenges in conserving the planet and make strong efforts to avoid excess and reduce waste. ☐

■ I contribute to groups and causes that work for peace in the world, for the reduction of poverty and hunger in the developing world, and for the promotion of a 'one world' future. ☐

Spiritual growth

■ I participate in activities that enhance my spiritual development such as:

– meditation on the 'big questions' ☐

– listening to inspiring and moving music ☐

– reading spiritually inspiring literature ☐

– working to create positives out of negatives ☐

– forgiving and asking for forgiveness ☐

– problem-solving and peace-making ☐

– activities that 'give back' to individuals and communities some of the things I have been lucky enough to receive ☐

– prayer. ☐

Total up your score and reflect on what that score might suggest to you.

The total possible is 100.

Scoring 0 to 30

Spirituality seems to play little part in your life at the moment. You seem to have no need of it or interest in it and can live your life happily without that dimension.

Scoring 31 to 69

You are engaged with spirituality and given opportunity and motivation might take your interests further. You might expand your exploration into areas or sources beyond those you currently relate to and benefit from doing so.

Scoring 70 to 100

You seem to have experience of, and great interest in, spirituality and it may already play a significant part in your life. You may accept the spiritual view that our development is limitless and will continue to advance your engagement with and pursuit of higher levels of spiritual awareness and application. Enjoy the journey!

[end activity]

After you've gone

In planning to make our lives more like we want them to be, we should apply all our awareness and skills to the task. There are no guarantees it will all work out, but it will certainly give us more of a chance of fulfilment. There is, of course, one thing that is true for all of us: 'no one gets out of here alive'. Hopefully, our lives will be stories of great relationships, memorable achievements, and significant happiness but, without being morbid, we are not going to last forever. It can help us order our future to reflect on what we would like our legacy to be when our time is up. What do we hope people will remember about us when we have gone? What will they say about us, about our qualities or otherwise, about our contribution to life?

In some sense this is a 'spiritual' question. We will not be 'around' in a physical sense, but we will have a presence in the minds and memories of many people: our partners, our children and grandchildren, our brothers, sisters, cousins, colleagues and certainly our friends.

Activity 7.2

My legacy

Let's imagine being able to sit in on a conversation about us, in a group gathered to remember us.

Who could be there? (think family, friends, colleagues etc.)

What would they say about:

■ Our character and personality?

_____

_____

■ Our qualities, strengths and weaknesses?

_____

_____

163

my work options

my finances

my relationships

my learning

my health and wellbeing

my leisure

my spirituality

■ The difference we made to their lives?

_____

_____

■ Our contribution to family?

_____

_____

■ Our contribution to friendships?

_____

_____

■ Our contribution to work life?

_____

_____

■ Our contribution to teams we were part of?

_____

_____

■ Our contribution to the wider community?

_____

_____

■ Our contribution to the wider world?

_____

_____

■ Our contribution to good causes?

_____

_____

■ Our contribution to the development of others?

_____

_____

■ What we will be best remembered for?

_____

_____

■ Our key achievements?

_____

_____

Listening in to this imaginary conversation, and the review of our life by those who had been spectators of it, how do you think we might feel?

How much of what is said might be about the *material* aspects of our life (the money, property, estate we had left) and how much about the more 'spiritual' dimension (our contribution to 'the spirit' of family relationships, to friendships, to community, to 'having left our world better than we found it, in some way')?

Are we living now with the priorities that will mean we are best remembered for those things we want to be remembered for? Do we need to change anything to make our legacy more like we would like it to be?

_____

_____

_____

_____

What are your reflections on this theme?

_____

_____

_____

_____

[end activity]

Finding out more

Web resources

- do an internet search on 'spiritual intelligence', 'types of intelligence', 'Maslow and spirituality', 'spirituality and health', 'religion and health', 'happiness', 'science of happiness', 'politics and happiness' and 'happiness research'
- www.spiritualprogressives.org
- www.yoursoulatwork.com
- For more information please visit www.fiftyforward.co.uk

Further reading

- *The Power of Spiritual Intelligence*, Tony Buzan (Thorsons London, 2001)
- *Your Soul at Work; How to live Your Values in the Workplace*, Bryan A Hiebert (Northstone Publishing Inc., 2005)
- Religion in Exile – *A Spiritual Homecoming*, Diarmuid O'Murchu (Crossroad Publishing Co. U.S., 2000)
- *Your Soul at Work*, Nicholas W Weiler, (Cowley Publications USA, 2003)
- *Anam Cara; Spiritual wisdom from the Celtic world*, John O'Donohue, Bantam Books, 1999

Summary

You have:

- Explored the dimensions of current views on spirituality
- Reflected on the part it may play in your life.

my work options

my finances

my relationships

my learning

my health and wellbeing

my leisure

my spirituality

my work options

my finances

my relationships

my learning

my health and wellbeing

my leisure

my spirituality

Action plans

Having worked on this section, looking at your own life so far and your plans for the next stage and looking towards your own legacy, is there anything;

■ You want to find out more about? _____

■ You want to begin to do differently? _____

■ You want to do more of or less of? _____

On the basis of those reflections write in what you would like more of, less of and what you would like to keep the same in the next phase of your life.

MORE OF…	LESS OF…	KEEP THE SAME

Choose three that you would like to start exploring now:

1. _____

2. _____

3. _____

> *'I don't believe there is one true religion, nor is there a heaven. Humanity is to make earth as close to our ideal of heaven as possible. Therefore, acts of kindness, charity and respect are everything. As Hillel said 'What is hateful to you, do not do to your neighbour; that is the whole Torah while the rest is commentary; go and learn it.'*
>
> *Shelley, in her 50s*

Life transitions

Introduction

John Lennon said, '*life is what happens to you when you are busy making plans*'. There are many things and events in life that we can predict, but there are others that take us by surprise and can dramatically impact our quality of life: an adult child dies, a partner wants a divorce after many years together, grandchildren suddenly require looking after because a parent cannot cope, goes to prison, chooses to work abroad; we have to face redundancy; we lose a pension etc. On the positive side, there may be an invitation to return to quality work again, long after this was expected; we may have unanticipated opportunities to travel; grandchildren arrive, after we had assumed that this was never going to happen; we rediscover old friends, who bring a new dimension to living, etc. These are all real-life examples from people we have interviewed.

We live in a culture where change, renewal and keeping up with the times matters like never before – and the over 50s are at the heart of this development.

Is *change* the same as *transition*?

No. Change is what happens to us – it's external; transition is how we deal with it – it's internal. A change can happen quite quickly, but its impact – the transition – may (and often does) take much longer. Changes can be frequent and minor. A transition can be, literally, life-changing; afterwards life will not be the same again.

If you have a good understanding of how transitions impact you, you will be much better equipped to deal with them. This section focuses on the process of transition – how it works. It also introduces the 'seven stages of a transition' in order to help you understand how they affect you. If we can understand the process of a transition, we can manage it more effectively.

Do you know?

- A person born in the earliest years of the twentieth century could expect to go through about eight major 'transitions' in their lifetime, and just one major 'life change' (in fact slightly less than one, on average) would happen after age 50. The average person born a generation later, in the 1930s or 40s, would have made eight major transitions by age 50 and might be on course for a total of twelve (four more major changes after age 50).

- It has been calculated that the average woman spends at least as many years caring for one or both parents as she did in caring for her children.

- Divorce rates have dropped by 8% over the last ten years – but have increased by over 20% in the over 60s.

- Research on 7,000 men and women by The Netherlands Institute of Mental Health and Addiction, shows that in the first year of bereavement almost 22% of the widowed experienced a major depression, 12% had symptoms of post-traumatic stress disorder and the rest had nine times more likelihood of developing an anxiety disorder.

The first half of life is about compulsion; the second half is about choice. Nature compels physical and cognitive maturation through early adulthood. Then the need to earn a place in society kicks in: education, career, family, status, recognition, and achievement. Once those are accomplished, it used to be time to die. Now more decades stretch ahead. Some people, to be sure, simply continue… without much reflection. But, for many, the old incentives no longer bite. They find themselves feeling uneasy. The questions I hear reflect the yearning and fear that comes with shedding old skin. 'Is this all there is?' 'Why don't I feel the passion and energy I once did?' 'Will the 1,300 weeks I have left just be a rehash?'… It's natural to grieve for a life that once felt right but no longer seems to make sense. For those who don't run and hide, exploring the new questions gradually leads to the realization that they have choices. The new awareness of "I can take my life in my own hands" is exhilarating.'

Professor Shosana Zuboff, founder of ODYSSEY: School for the Second Half of Life – a unique executive program at the Harvard Business School devoted to the issues of midlife transition

From our own experiences on career management workshops of working with people reviewing their lives, we recall examples of the 50-year-old senior manager from ICI who left to become a flautist in a Brazilian symphony orchestra; the chemistry teacher who set up the most northern vineyard in the UK; the pilot and his wife who set off to spend the rest of their lives travelling and working around the world; the senior manager who 'gave it all up' and went to live and work in the vineyards of the Dordogne, the successful engineer who decided to take up dry stone walling as his new career, after 60 – and so on.

Activity 1

The seven stages of a transition

Knowing where you are in a transition, knowing that your feelings will pass (and knowing that your feelings are normal and that many others experience them) will help you manage what is happening when significant change hits you, and help you move through the transition more easily.

Our feelings, during a transition, tend to fall into seven stages. It is important to remember that we will need to go through all seven stages before the transition process is complete. Some of the stages may be very brief, but we will go through them in one form or another.

Changes in Self-Esteem During Transitions

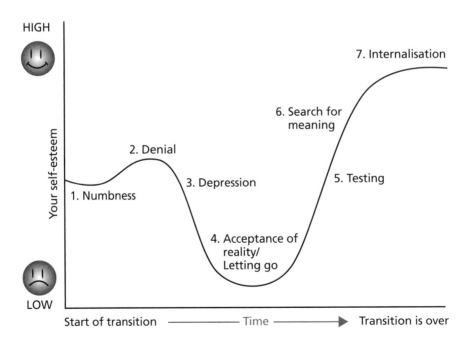

Part 1

The seven stages: what are they and what do they mean?

After reading each explanation, try to remember a time when you were in a transition and have felt like that.

Stage 1: Numbness

The first phase is sometimes described as shock. It is a sense of being overwhelmed; of being unable to make plans, unable to reason, and unable to understand. In other words, you freeze up. The more unfamiliar the transition, the stronger this feeling is. In bereavement, for example, many people feel strange because of the absence of feeling; but it is normal to feel numb at this stage of a transition. However, if you feel positive about the transition, as you might feel positive about getting married, this stage will be less intense.

An example of this in my life was:

_____

_____

Stage 2: Denial

The movement from numbness to the second stage of denial does not feel greatly different at the time it is happening. This is because we try to make the transition seem less important or argue that it won't affect us. Very often we will attempt to deny that a transition even exists!

During this stage people may feel 'This is not as bad as I expected' or 'Things will soon be back to normal'. This is often because the body is building up its defences for the full impact of the change, which is yet to come. At this stage the person may feel highly energetic because, with a transition such as bereavement, the person is often at the centre of attention from their friends and relatives, there are things to be done and dealt with. With a change such as a new job, the denial stage may be a refusal to recognise some of the real changes that will take place, for example the loss of old workmates, new responsibilities and the uncertainty about being able to do the new job.

An example of this in my life was:

_____

_____

Stage 3: Depression/self-doubt

Eventually, for most people, the realities of the transition, and of the stress that comes with it, begin to become clear. As people become aware that they must make some changes in the way they are living, as they become aware of the realities involved, they sometimes become uncertain. Self-doubt is usually a consequence of feelings of powerlessness, of aspects of life being out of our control. This can happen even when we are really looking forward to a change, not only when it is feared. So, getting that dream job, for example, can lead to doubts about being capable of doing the job, having to move, making new friends, etc

In this stage the person can have periods of high energy, which can sometimes show itself as anger, before sliding back into a feeling of hopelessness. They may become frustrated, because it seems difficult to know how best to cope with the new life situation, the new ways of being and the new relationships that have been established.

An example of this in my life was:

_____

_____

Stage 4: Letting go

As people gradually become aware of their reality, they can move into the fourth phase, which is accepting the situation for what it is. Letting go may be a gradual 'three steps forward – two steps back' type of process. This may be quite painful and makes them think 'This is awful. I thought I was through this, but I'm not.'

To move from phase three to phase four involves a process of unhooking from the past and saying 'Well, here I am now, this is what I have and I know I can survive. I may not be sure of what I want yet, but I will be OK.' Once the new reality or situation has been accepted, the person begins to feel optimistic.

An example of this in my life was:

_____

_____

Stage 5: Testing

The person becomes much more active and starts testing him or herself in the new situation, trying out new behaviours and new ways of coping with the change. After divorce, for example, this is often a stage when people begin dating again. There is a lot of personal energy available during this phase and it sometimes shows itself in irritation, or tears.

An example of this in my life was:

_____

_____

Stage 6: Search for meaning

Following the burst of activity and self-testing, there is a gradual shift towards *understanding* – when the person may ask, 'Is this right for me?' or 'What does this mean for me?'. We need to know what the changes mean to us and how they will affect our future. If the change is not 'right for us', then there will be further testing of alternatives, until one is found that seems to fit. It is only when we have a sense of what these changes mean, and what their meaning for our life is, that we can move on to the final stage.

An example of this in my life was:

_____

_____

Stage 7: Internalisation or acceptance

At last, if we have been able to accept the transition, we move into the final phase of internalisation. This is when we take all the effects of the transition and make them part of our lives or routines. When we have fully accepted (internalised) the stages of the transition that we have been through, then we can begin to look forward in a more positive frame of mind and start to build on the new strengths we have developed.

An example of this in my life was:

_____

_____

Rarely, if ever, does a person move neatly from phase to phase. For example, one person may never get beyond denial. Another may just stop at depression. Sometimes we may feel that we are over something and then something happens which takes us back. It can feel like that it is 3 steps forward and 2 steps back. One person that we knew who had just lived through a difficult divorce was convinced that he had 'got over her' – until he saw her, for the first time, out with another man. The important realisation is that overall it is still one step forward and we should press on.

But, for a transition to be effectively managed, all seven phases need to be worked through. Often we try to avoid the depression stage, or help others avoid it, but only when we allow ourselves or others to grieve can we move towards the new opportunities opened up to us by the change. Understanding the process of change and the stages of transition will help you to cope with your feelings and move forward.

Part 2

Now think back to some of the bigger transitions that you have faced in your life. Choose two that were particularly important to you. Try to choose two with different characteristics: for example, one you felt good about and one that involved change that was difficult to accept.

My two transitions are:

1. _____

2. _____

With these in mind, answer the following questions.

Transition 1:

1. Numbness

■ What was your first reaction?

_____

_____

■ How did you know the transition had started?

_____

_____

■ What did you feel/do?

_____

_____

2. Denial

■ How did you try to minimise or deny the transition?

_____

_____

3. Depression/self-doubt

■ Did you doubt your ability to handle the transition? Why?

_____

_____

- ■ What did this make you feel/do?

_____

_____

4. Letting go

- ■ When did you realise the transition was inevitable?

_____

_____

- ■ How did it feel to accept the change?

_____

_____

5. Testing

- ■ What did you do to test out the transition?

_____

_____

6. Search for meaning

- ■ What was the meaning of this transition for you?

_____

_____

7. Acceptance

- ■ Looking back, what did you think about your experience of transition?

_____

_____

Transition 2:

1. Numbness

- ■ What was your first reaction?

_____

_____

- ■ How did you know the transition had started?

_____

_____

- What did you feel/do?

_____

_____

2. Denial

- How did you try to minimise or deny the transition?

_____

_____

3. Depression/self-doubt

- Did you doubt your ability to handle the transition? Why?

_____

_____

- What did this make you feel/do?

_____

_____

4. Letting go

- When did you realise the transition was inevitable?

_____

_____

- How did it feel to accept the change?

_____

_____

5. Testing

- What did you do to test out the transition?

_____

_____

6. Search for meaning

- What was the meaning of this transition for you?

_____

_____

7. Acceptance

■ Looking back, what did you think about your experience of transition?

_____

_____

By considering these two transitions you have started to build up a picture of how you deal with them. What have you learned about how you deal with transitions?

_____

_____

_____

_____

_____

_____

[end activity]

Life is a series of challenges for each of us – whether we like it or not! Some people enjoy stability and like things to remain constant. Others of us are only happy when we are on the move. But, whoever you are, it is inevitable that you will be faced with major events in your life that will almost certainly lead to transitions.

Many people are afraid of change and transitions. They are filled with a sense of unease when faced with change in their lives, jobs or careers. But transitions are not all negative. Many of them are extremely enjoyable or have positive results. Even transitions which appear negative on the surface can turn out to be enjoyable or at least valuable learning experiences.

> _'Losing my arm at 21. It made me a stronger character with great determination but most of all it made me realise what was and was not important in life.'_
>
> Chris Read, in his 60s

So, the first trick of good transition management is to learn to look on every transition, every challenge, not as a potential problem, but as an opportunity to make something positive happen in your life.

> _'Death of father resulted in reconnecting with brother and 3 nephews after 15 years of separation – massive at the time but more good things than bad have distilled from the haze.'_
>
> Klaus, in his 50s

> _'My father's death at 62 gave me my first focus on what did I want out of my working life; my early thoughts about retirement were formed.'_
>
> Ian Walker, in his 50s

We will now give you some suggestions on how you can develop skills to enable you to take the worry and stress out of transitions. It also includes preparing for transitions and some common barriers to dealing with transitions effectively.

Being proactive

Often we do not choose a transition. This sometimes makes it difficult for us to accept it, but basically we have only three choices:

- refuse to accept it
- accept it, but just 'put up' with it
- accept it and try to benefit from it.

The first will bring nothing but bad feelings and is unlikely to reverse the transition. It will probably mean that we are unable to cope with the tasks facing us in the new situation. The second will help us survive. The third will help us not only to survive but to benefit and grow from the experience.

It sometimes helps you to face your fears by asking 'What is the worst thing that can happen?' Our anxieties are usually based upon vague and fantastic fears. Actually facing up to the worst that can happen may help us to identify possibilities. If we think and talk about these possibilities, we will probably find that they are not that terrible, or that they are unlikely to happen. Even if the worst does happen, at least we have prepared ourselves for it.

'Making things happen' in the way you want them to, rather than waiting for things to happen to you, is being proactive. It is an approach which stems from a belief that you can always make things 'more like you want them to be'; that you can be more 'in charge' of yourself and situations; that you can be someone who does things for yourself rather than someone who has things done to you. It is not about being aggressive, but rather about choosing, acting and growing positively. The more you are thinking, deciding and doing for yourself the more useful you are going to be to yourself and to the people around you.

All transitions involve making decisions: sometimes easy, sometimes painful. Letting other people make decisions for you does not help you to manage your transition and grow in the ways that you want. However, there are a number of things you can do which can help you be more proactive and feel more in control. They include:

- Physical wellbeing
- Relaxation
- Regular routine
- Knowing others who can help you
- Managing your transitions one at a time
- Not blaming or punishing yourself
- Managing your decisions one at a time
- Remembering that time will help.

Let's look at these in a little more detail.

- **Physical wellbeing**

    Our ability to cope with stress depends on our physical wellbeing. We need to be fit and well to cope with transitions, so exercise and eating regularly and wisely are essential coping skills. It is particularly important to eat well during a transition when you may have neither the time nor the inclination to do so.

- **Relaxation**

    Relaxation techniques are also well worth learning, as they can help prevent you from becoming too uptight about things that are bothering you. Make a point of spending a little time relaxing each day. It sometimes helps to give yourself a treat – an outing to a favourite peaceful spot; a visit to the hairdresser, or to a friend; or buying yourself something small that you will enjoy.

- **Regular routine**

    Routine and structure in your life can be of great assistance at times of change. Look for the 'anchor points' in your life, the stable areas that remain the same even when all else is changing. These include the basic routines, such as going to bed at a regular hour, eating meals, shopping and work outside or in the home. These are trivial events but can be a lifeline during difficult periods.

- **Knowing others who can help you**

    There is now considerable evidence to show that talking problems through with people helps to reduce stress at times of change. Having a support group is a valuable asset. Your own support group could include your partner, parents, relatives, friends, and so on (see Activity 3.1 in 'My relationships'). It is important to develop a range of 'helpers' rather than being dependent on just one or two people for everything. Obviously, most of our support comes from friends or those sympathetic to us, but it is also important to be challenged. Someone who can make us face up to things can actually provoke us into examining our ideas and actions in a very positive way.

- **Manage your transitions one at a time**

    This might be easier said than done, as some major life events may involve several changes. For example, a move to a new home can also mean, as well as the search for suitable accommodation, adapting to new patterns of travel, finding new centres for shopping and leisure, a new job, and making new friends and contacts. It will help you if you can identify each transition and deal with each separately, one at a time. Many of us are tempted to change everything in one go. Sheila got divorced and decided that this was the time to sell the house, get a new job and move. Unless you have to this is definitely not a good idea and the research on life changes and health strongly support this. See Activity 8.2.

- **Don't blame yourself or punish yourself**

  When things go wrong, as they are bound to sometimes, don't waste time in destructive self-criticism. This just undermines your self-esteem even further. Take time out to think about the new situation and how best to deal with it; give yourself a little treat to boost your self-esteem and you will be surprised how much easier it is to deal with whatever you feel has gone wrong.

- **Manage your decisions one at a time**

  It is surprising how many decisions can be safely postponed until you feel better able to make them. This is not the same as letting events or other people make your decisions for you, or dodging the whole issue and putting it off indefinitely. Rather, it is the clever knack of recognising which decisions have the highest priority and must be dealt with now, and which decisions can safely wait until you have more information, or until a decision has become absolutely necessary.

  Don't let other people push you into making a decision you do not feel ready to make. If necessary, tell yourself and other people that you are busy dealing with another decision which must come first, and that you will deal with the next one when you are ready. This is called 'planned procrastination'.

- **Remember that time will help**

  Time will help you come to terms with any new situation. But in order to come through a transition feeling that you have learned from the experience, you need to help yourself along the way. All of the reading and the thinking that you are doing now will help you to manage the transition in a proactive way – for yourself.

The impact of transitions

In the 1940s and 1950s, Drs Thomas Holmes and Richard Rahe developed the concept that the onset of illness can be related to life stress. They developed a scale of 43 life events, and standardised them by asking many subjects to rank them by the amount of readjustment required, regardless of desirability.

This scale was then studied in several groups, including navy seamen in the US and Norway, and underwater demolition teams. In addition, it has been studied in patients suffering from depression, heart attacks, tuberculosis, fractures, accidents, duodenal ulcers, as well as in athletes.

The general findings are consistent in both types of studies, across a variety of cultures and populations. The higher the score, the higher the likelihood of illness occurring in the following six months. Higher scores also correlate with more severe illnesses. The assessment tool is called the **Social Readjustment Rating Scale** or sometimes the **Life Changes Units Scale**.[24] This can give you an estimate of your likelihood of developing minor or major physical disease, according to how many life changes you have experienced over the past 12 months.

24 Holmes & Rahe (1967), Holmes-Rahe life changes scale, *Journal of Psychosomatic Research*, Vol. 11, pp. 213–218.

Activity 2

Do transitions make us sick?

Look at the list of life changes outlined in the table below. Ask yourself how many you have experienced over the 12 months and tick them. Each life change has a score. Note that simply getting through Christmas gets you 12 points!

Life Experience	Life Change Units
death of spouse	100
divorce	73
marital separation	65
jail term	63
death of close family member	63
personal injury or illness	53
marriage	50
fired at work	47
marital reconciliation	45
retirement	45
change in health of family member	44
pregnancy	40
sex difficulties	39
gain of new family member	39
business readjustment	39
change in financial state	38
death of close friend	37
change to different line of work	36
change in number of arguments with spouse	35
mortgage or loan over £10,000 ('large loan')	31
foreclosure of mortgage or loan	30
change in responsibilities at work	29
son or daughter leaving home	29
trouble with in-laws	29
outstanding personal achievement	28
spouse begins or stops work	26
begin or end school	26
change in living conditions	25
revision of personal habits	24
trouble with boss	23
change in work hours or conditions	20
change in residence	20
change in schools	20

Life Experience	Life Change Units
change in recreation	19
change in church activities	19
change in social activities	18
mortgage or loan less than £10,000 ('small loan')	17
change in sleeping habit	16
change in number of family get-togethers	15
change in eating habits	15
vacation	13
Christmas	12
minor violations of the law	11

Add up the total number of points.

Write your total here _____

[end activity]

What does your score mean?

- 0–149 – very little life change – good health
- 150–199 – mild life change – risk of colds, flu, occasional depression
- 200–249 – moderate life change – depression
- 250–299 – serious life change – risk of lowered resistance to disease
- 300–999 – major life change – risk of major illness within two years

Probability of illness

The Life Changes Units Scale is not an absolute predictor of illness in the next two years, but empirically the researchers have found a strong statistical prediction.

LCU score	Probability of illness in two years
150–199	37%
200–299	51%
>300	79%

Remember:

- Some transitions might seem to be 'good' for the person (job promotion, marriage) and others might seem 'bad' (death of close family member, divorce).
- Some people may be good at adapting to high levels of transition and thrive at higher levels than average – in those people, a recent increase in LCU score may predict illness more accurately than their 'baseline' score.
- In general, women seem to rate life events as more stressful than men do; older people tend to rate life events as less stressful than younger people rate them.

Finding out more

Chat rooms could be especially useful here in identifying one or more people who have experienced a similar transition to your own. How have they dealt with it? Are they having difficulties that you may be able to help them with?

Try the mentoring part of **www.fiftyforward .co.uk**.

There are often support groups to help people work their way through a major life transition, in particular bereavement, divorce, death of a child, being a victim of crime, living with someone with a major physical or mental illness, caring for elderly parents, etc. Whatever the transition, type the name of it into a search engine to explore a range of options.

Summary

- You should now understand the nature of transitions and how they can affect your life.

- You understand the process of transition and know that there are seven stages through which you must pass: numbness, minimisation, depression/self-doubt, acceptance of reality/letting go, testing, search for meaning, internalisation.

- You are aware of the stress you may face during a transition and you now know ways of coping with it.

- You know that a transition presents opportunities for you if you can identify them.

Use this knowledge whenever you face a major transition in your life and, as you already know, things will become easier.

Action plans

In the space below, write down three things you have learnt about yourself in this section:

1. _____

2. _____

3. _____

Now identify three things you will do in the future to improve your transition management skills:

1. _____

2. _____

3. _____

> 'Well, being told my marriage was over was a great shock... I often refer to the years from 1991–6 as 'my forgotten years'. I had to lick my wounds and get on with life. In '96 I sold my flat, rented for six months and bought a cottage in the Cotswolds. I wanted to re-connect with a community and the past ten years have been some of the most fulfilling times of my life!'
>
> *John Cull, in his 50s*

Notes

Bringing it all together: where do you go from here?

Introduction

An article, 'What do the over 50s really want?'[25], by Jayne Warren reported on a 'wish-list' published by the government to celebrate 'UK Older People's Day'. The list claims to be the 'ultimate wish list of 60 goals for the over 50s' and claims to provide new insights into the upbeat ambitions of older people in the first decade of the twenty-first century.[26]

The goals reported are extremely varied (e.g. 'learning to cook', 'go on a wine tasting course', 'make a scrapbook of childhood', 'learn to play a musical instrument', 'take up painting', 'design a garden', 'go to the 2012 London Olympics', 'run a marathon', 'have more sex', 'see the northern lights', 'see an opera', 'telling someone you love them everyday', 'volunteering' etc.) and challenging (e.g. 'hang gliding', 'taking flying lessons', 'swimming with dolphins').

The evidence is that we over 50s are greatly optimistic about the second half of our lives, and we are ambitious, energetic and purposeful. Sir Terry Wogan summed up the generational philosophy very well, when he pointed out 'Use-by dates don't apply to people!'

As you have worked through the different sections of this book, you will have been accumulating lots of information about your thoughts on work and life, the changes you want to make and the goals and ambitions you want to pursue. You will have become more aware of what is important to you, what you want to be different and what you might need to do to make aspects of your life more like you want them to be.

It's time now to review all your work, to re-visit all the **'More of… Less of…'** tables at the end of each theme and your **Aha!** pages, and ask yourself:

'Where do I go from here?

What am I going to do that will get me from here to where I want to be?'

Spend some time doing this! There will be a great deal of material there. You may already have listed some action plans at the end of the sections you have worked through.

As you review the work you have done, reflect and ask yourself the following questions:

- What is the picture I have built up about my life so far; about the skills, strengths, knowledge and experiences I have to carry me into the next phase of my life?

- What are the hopes and ambitions I have for the time ahead?

- What balance or priorities am I looking for in my different life roles?

- What are the challenges that lie ahead that I will address?

- What are the issues and intentions my work on the Life Themes has produced for me?

- What do I feel most motivated about at this stage?

- How will I build my rainbow?

You need to pull together the full picture and identify what you want to make happen in the next phase of your life and career.

You will probably have worked with a mind map[27] in Theme 1 about your retirement. We think that it is such a useful whole brain tool that we are suggesting that you use it again here.

25 *What Do The Over 50s Really Want?*, Jayne Warren, http://maturetimes.co.uk, October 2007.

26 You can see the full list by logging on to the website www.fiftyforward.co.uk. Look under the 'Start' heading, then hit '50+ fabulous' and then 'Liven up your leisure time'.

27 See www.buzanworld.com – this website describes the work and ideas of Tony Buzan and offers a free trial of software for making Mind Maps.

Here is just one example of a mind map made by somebody working with their material – but note that, although there are certain principles to creating a mind map, the end result will vary dramatically from person to person. It's also worth pointing out that people never get it 'right' first off – they inevitably start too far to the centre/top/right/bottom/left – because you never know where the map is going to take you. If you intend to make your map a work of art, and prettify and beautify it, then we'd suggest you draft it first!

Career and Life Mind Map

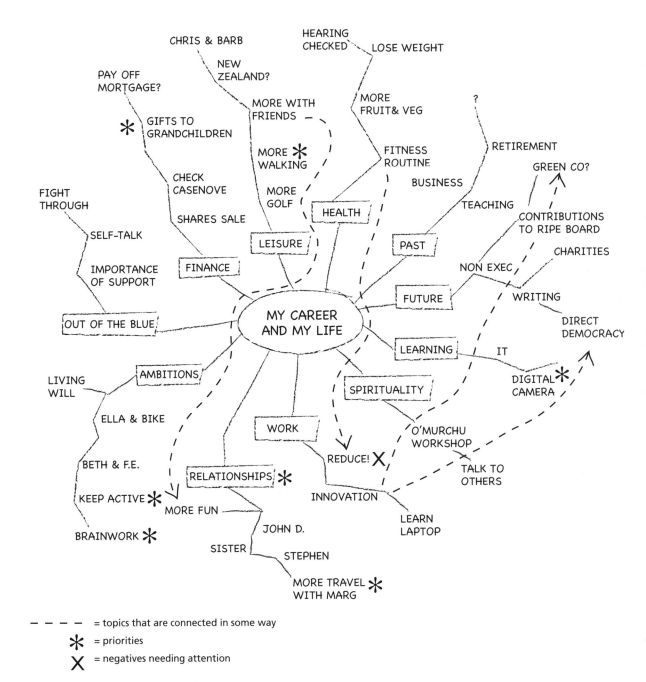

- - - - = topics that are connected in some way

✳ = priorities

✗ = negatives needing attention

Activity 1

My career and my life mind map

Working on a large sheet of paper, at least A3, put the **title** of your mind map right at the centre – *'My career and my life'* (see example).

Add the heading for the first of the **themes** you will think through – think in terms of branch lines leaving a main line station and heading outwards to suburbs. Start anywhere with any theme.

Write in the theme heading in capitals or perhaps use different colours.

Reflecting on the relevant areas you have worked on, let your mind flow around each theme and develop the line leading outwards. As thoughts come to mind, enter the **key words** or **details** on the line.

Think through and build your mind map around the different themes you have worked on or any other theme of your life or career that you wish to think through. Take your time, it is valuable work!

When you have 'completed' your mind map, study it carefully and as you do, consider the following:

■ Looking at the whole map where are the satisfiers for me – the things that bring me satisfaction and happiness? (*Mark these with a '*✱*'.*)

■ Where are the dissatisfactions for me – the things I would like less of or like to change? (*Mark these with an 'X'?*)

■ Are there things that link up and can be addressed together? (*Draw in any links.*)

■ Is there anything missing that should be on there? *If so, add it now.*

Now answer the following questions:

■ What are the most important messages for me from this picture as I contemplate the next phase of my life and career?

_____

_____

_____

■ What are the things I most want to do something about?

_____

_____

_____

■ Are there any surprises for me on my mind map? If so, what are they?

_____

_____

_____

■ Which areas of my life and career require my attention and action as a priority?

_____

_____

_____

■ What differences am I looking for in each of the areas of my life and career that I have worked on?

_____

_____

_____

■ Who are the key people in my life and career?

_____

_____

_____

■ What are the relationships I wish to work on?

_____

_____

_____

■ Where do I get the support I need and how might I make best use of that?

_____

_____

_____

Now summarise what you want in the following matrix.

On the basis of your reflections on the material you have produced, note your priorities on this matrix. What would like you more of, less of and what you would like to keep the same in your life right now?

	More of...	Less of...	Keep the same
My work options			
My finances			
My relationships			
My learning			
My health and wellbeing			
My leisure			
My spirituality			

Choose three of your entries that it is most important for you to start working on right now:

1. _____

2. _____

3. _____

[end activity]

We're getting towards the end of the journey, so this is time to take stock of everything you have been considering as you have worked through the book. You've just recorded your three priorities, and the next activity allows you to make some definite plans to make them happen.

> *'If you don't know where you are going you could finish up somewhere else!'*
> *Anon.*

Activity 2

Setting objectives

What are the three most important things you want to work on?

Part 1

Take each of these in turn and work through the following steps to identify clear objectives that will help you achieve what you are seeking.

■ State each objective clearly by starting with the word 'To _____ ', and following this with an action word. (E.g. '**To** *take a course in web design* **in order to** *further my skills and increase my options*.')

1. _____

2. _____

3. _____

■ Ask yourself whether there is a prior objective that needs to come before your main objective (e.g. 'To do a web search for web design courses available in my area'). If so, note it here.

_____

_____

_____

Working again on each objective, complete the following.

■ State clearly how you will know when each objective has been achieved (e.g. 'In September when I complete the course and receive the certificate.')

_____

_____

_____

■ Make sure each objective is absolutely specific (e.g. 'To complete a course on Adobe Dreamweaver and Flash CS3').

_____

_____

_____

■ Check that each objective is something YOU want to achieve – setting objectives for other people can lead to great frustration. (e.g. 'To ask a friend to make enquiries for me about courses in the area'. Don't let your objectives be reliant on somebody else.)

■ Avoid Catch 22! Check that none of your objectives clash with each other – that way lies confusion for you – and possibly others!

■ Think through the consequences there might be, if any, if you pursue each objective. Are these acceptable to you or do you need to re-think?

- Identify any barriers or constraints that may lie in the way of your objective – you may have to deal with some things first.
- Identify where you can get support for your objective that will help you in achieving it.

Part 2

Check that each objective passes the SMART test. Is it:

- **S**pecific: absolutely clearly stated
- **M**easurable: you will know clearly when you have achieved it
- **A**chievable: whilst being ambitious you are not striving for the unattainable
- **R**ealistic: you truly believe you can do it and are motivated to do so
- **T**imely: it has a clearly stated timeframe (e.g. 'within 30 days' or 'by the end of the year' etc.) and you have the time to commit to its achievement ?

Work on each of your three priority objectives. Get them through the SMART test and list them here.

1. _____

2. _____

3. _____

[end activity]

> '*We fail to achieve things we want for two reasons. Either our action plan is not good enough or we are not sufficiently motivated!*'
>
> *Anon.*

- An **Objective** is something we *WANT* and *AIM* to achieve.
- An **Action Plan** is *WHAT* we will do and *WHEN* to achieve it.

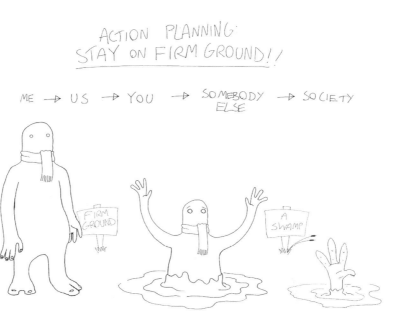

The illustration warns us of the dangers of making loose, woolly, vague or remote action plans. The further we get from doing things OURSELVES and TODAY, the more likely our plans will sink in the swamp!

Activity 3

Action planning

■ Identify the objective you want to work on first.

_____

_____

■ Write down what YOU are going to do about it and WHEN.

_____

_____

Stay out of the Swamp!

■ Build up the Action Steps you will need to take in sequence to achieve the objective.

_____

_____

■ Make sure each of the steps you take is absolutely specific and timed.

_____

_____

Decide when you will review progress and readjust your action plans as necessary.

Work on your action plans for each objective. Decide priorities and action sequences and put your initial action steps into your diary.

[end activity]

If at first we don't succeed...

It is important to be highly motivated if we wish to change the features of our life and our career that we want to be different. However, we live in a complex world and we are involved and interact with other unique individuals. Not everything we set our heart on may be achieved and it will be important on those occasions to draw back for a while and think again. Some would say that it is always sensible to have a Plan B, even as we are working on Plan A.

However, what if we come up against a situation we wish to be different – and find that our efforts don't get us the results that we want? In that situation it is important to recognise we have some options. We can do any of the following.

- **Try again to change things:** revise our action plan, re-commit – and who knows what difference persistence might make?

- **Leave it:** if something is very much not to our liking, if we have tried everything to change it without success, we can move out, move away, move on. Fresh starts, if chosen, well-judged and prepared for, can be fruitful.

- **Change ourselves:** if _leaving_ is not possible or not to our liking then we can _change ourselves_ to make things better. We can change how we see things, change our ideas, change our focus, change our priorities, change how we deal with things. Changing ourselves can change other people and change how we experience situations.

- **Live with it:** this means more than just shrugging our shoulders and surrendering. We can live more successfully with a situation we wish were different by focusing less on it and more on something else, by reducing the 'space' we give it in our thoughts or in our day. We can find attractive distractions that take our minds off the problem and reduce its significance, we can use our support system to 'get stuff off our chests', to 'share the problem', to 'give ourselves a break', to learn to laugh at ourselves or the world. Security means always having an alternative!

Involving others

We do not live in a vacuum. Our thoughts, our actions, our plans are likely to have implications for and impact on others; partners, families, friends, colleagues may be affected by our decisions and new directions.

While we have been focusing on _our_ future, others have been attending to _their_ present. They may be curious as to what we have been doing and what we may have in mind. We owe it to people who are special or important to us to share the experience – and the possible outcomes.

Activity 4

Putting others in the picture

- Who do you need to speak to about your experience of this process and the plans you are emerging with?

  _____

  _____

- How are they likely to be affected by, and react to, what you are intent upon?

  _____

  _____

- What are the outcomes you want?

  _____

  _____

- What will be the best way to put them in the picture? When, where, how?

  _____

  _____

- What are your action plans?

  _____

  _____

[end activity]

On the workshops we used to run, we always found that a very effective technique at this stage was to ask participants to write a letter to themselves, which we would post on to them in six months. We can't promise that to readers of this book, but the device is a valuable one. Almost certainly, when the time comes, you will have forgotten all about it – but it can be fun and useful to get a reminder of our intentions and ambitions and see how we have progressed our plans or how we may need to re-assess them.

Activity 5

A letter to yourself

With current technology it is possible to send an email to yourself if you visit **www.bored.com/emailcapsules**, and you can choose any date in the future that you wish. Or you could leave a note in an electronic calendar for a future date, possibly with a computer file link to the letter.

If you prefer the old technology, we invite you to write a letter to yourself and file it away to be opened in six months time. Enter in your diary a reminder in six months time to retrieve that letter and check your progress (remember to note where it is filed!). Your letter should spell out clearly what you hope to have achieved for each of your three priority objectives in the next six months.

[end activity]

We truly hope that by this stage you will have demonstrated to yourself that you really *can* create your own future. By combining awareness and skills, you can make the second half of your life more like you want it to be.

Remember, luck is the crossroads where preparation and opportunity meet. Our objective for this programme has been to get you to that crossroads and for you to visualise, plan and act to set off in the direction that is right for you and for those closest to you.

Some final thoughts

> *'Once you are 65, you realise that life is too short. I made a vow about people I won't see, work I don't really want to do, bad restaurants I won't eat in. I want to be able to say, 'If yesterday was the last day of my life, did I throw it away?'*
>
> *Nora Ephron, film director and author*

So, you have given time and attention to your life and career review. Hopefully you have emerged with a clearer sense of direction and purpose, a motivation to make it happen and a well-worked set of action plans.

This process has been used by literally thousands of people over the last 30 years. They have:

- Used the reflection time to review where they are and found that they can often return with a new commitment to their lives

- Used the process to make very dramatic changes and reported over the years their appreciation of the momentum it gave them

- Invited partners to experience the process themselves so that they do not feel 'left behind' in the 'out-of-stepness' that can result if only one of a partnership is involved

- Used the 'tools' that the process provides at subsequent times in their lives, when they sense they are outgrowing (as we all do) their current life phase or job and need a new direction.

Below are the most important messages about the process and the website:

- Make them your servant and not your master. Do not let anything you have read or done dictate to you.

- Take charge of the material you have produced, own it, set objectives for what you want to be different, commit to the actions you decide to take.

- Be clear that the most important elements in the process are you and those you care about; be sensitive as well as motivated.

- Stay in charge of yourself, your situations and your decisions.

- Be prepared to adapt and reshape your plans; not everything will work out exactly as we wish.

- Get plenty of support and encouragement and give that back to those who need it from you.

This is your life, it is yours to shape and be in charge of!

You really can create your own future and continue to build rainbows for yourself and for others.

Barrie Hopson and *Mike Scally*

> *'Life's journey is not to arrive at the grave safely in a well-preserved body, but rather to skid in sideways, totally worn out, shouting, "Holy shit…What a Ride!!" '*
>
> *Mavis Leyrer, 87*

Notes

Appendices

APPENDIX 1

Life value cards

Ambition *You aspire to high achievement, status or standing.*	**Integrity** *You are committed to honesty and high moral standards.*
Relationships *You place high importance on the quality and maintenance of your relationships with friends and family.*	**Helping society** *You like to be involved in things which will make a contribution to the community, society or the world.*
Artistic *You appreciate art, music, design, books, theatre, film, etc.*	**Reputation** *You prize being held in high esteem for your qualities and achievements.*
Work–life balance *You want a balance between your paid work and all the other areas of your life.*	**Spirituality** *You have a sense of and commitment to 'a greater good', to a better world, to a common humanity, to a just and healthy society, to a planet at peace.*
Contact with people *You enjoy having a lot of contact and interaction with people.*	**Health and wellbeing** *You are committed to a lifestyle which best ensures your physical and mental wellbeing.*

Stability

You value permanence and continuity in your relationships and your activities.

Teamwork

You like working with others and collective achievement.

Excitement

You need a lot of excitement in your life.

Physical challenge

You enjoy doing something that is physically demanding.

Pleasure

The 'good things of life', fun and enjoyment and time for them matter a great deal to you.

Making decisions

You like making decisions about how things should be done, who should do it and by when.

Community

You like living in a place that gives you ready access to activities and people you value (e.g. social contacts, leisure, learning, entertainment, church, etc.)

Challenge

You like being stretched, adventure, new ground, responding to the unexpected.

Independence

You like being independent, a free agent, in charge of your own life and options.

Wealth

It matters to you to have a healthy bank balance and significant assets.

Learning

It is important to you to continually learn new things.

Being expert

You like being known as someone with special knowledge or skills.

Helping others

You like to help other people individually or in groups.

Persuading people

You enjoy persuading people to change their minds, buy something, volunteer for something, etc.

Security

You like to live free of fear or anxiety with few financial worries in a safe, unthreatening environment.

Risk

You like to take physical, financial, emotional or intellectual risks.

Peace

You prefer to have few pressures or uncomfortable demands.

Communication

You enjoy being able to express ideas well in writing or in speech.

Time freedom

You prefer to be able to choose your own times for doing things.

Creative

Thinking up new ideas and ways of doing, expressing or representing things is important to you.

Competition

You like competing against other people or groups.

Variety

You like to have lots of different things to do and frequent change.

Very Important

This is very important to me and drives many of my decisions and actions.

Important

This is important to me and definitely affects what I decide and what I do.

Quite Important

This is quite important to me and shapes some of my decisions

Of Little Importance

This is of little importance to me.

Not Important

This is not one of my values and has no influence on what I pursue or how I operate.

APPENDIX 2

2.1: My life values

VERY IMPORTANT
1
2
3
4
5
6
7
8

MY NOT IMPORTANT VALUES
1
2
3
4
5
6
7
8

2.2: My job and my values

Very important	My present job	Job alternative no. 1	Job alternative no. 2
1	_ X 8 =	_ X 8 =	_ X 8 =
2	_ X 7 =	_ X 7 =	_ X 7 =
3	_ X 6 =	_ X 6 =	_ X 6 =
4	_ X 5 =	_ X 5 =	_ X 5 =
5	_ X 4 =	_ X 4 =	_ X 4 =
6	_ X 3 =	_ X 3 =	_ X 3 =
7	_ X 2 =	_ X 2 =	_ X 2 =
8	_ X 1 =	_ X 1 =	_ X 1 =
	TOTAL:	TOTAL:	TOTAL:
MY *NOT IMPORTANT* CARDS ARE:	Tick any of these if they feature in your present job or any alternative jobs		
1			
2			
3			
4			
5			
6			
7			
8			

2.3: My unpaid work and my values

Very important	Activity 1	Activity 2	Activity 3
1	_ X 8 =	_ X 8 =	_ X 8 =
2	_ X 7 =	_ X 7 =	_ X 7 =
3	_ X 6 =	_ X 6 =	_ X 6 =
4	_ X 5 =	_ X 5 =	_ X 5 =
5	_ X 4 =	_ X 4 =	_ X 4 =
6	_ X 3 =	_ X 3 =	_ X 3 =
7	_ X 2 =	_ X 2 =	_ X 2 =
8	_ X 1 =	_ X 1 =	_ X 1 =
	TOTAL:	TOTAL:	TOTAL:
MY *NOT IMPORTANT* CARDS ARE:	Tick any of these if they feature in any activity		
1			
2			
3			
4			
5			
6			
7			
8			

2.4: Patterns of employment and my values

Very important	My present pattern	Alternative no. 1	Alternative no. 2
1	_ X 8 =	_ X 8 =	_ X 8 =
2	_ X 7 =	_ X 7 =	_ X 7 =
3	_ X 6 =	_ X 6 =	_ X 6 =
4	_ X 5 =	_ X 5 =	_ X 5 =
5	_ X 4 =	_ X 4 =	_ X 4 =
6	_ X 3 =	_ X 3 =	_ X 3 =
7	_ X 2 =	_ X 2 =	_ X 2 =
8	_ X 1 =	_ X 1 =	_ X 1 =
	TOTAL:	TOTAL:	TOTAL:
MY *NOT IMPORTANT* CARDS ARE:	Tick any of these if they feature in your current job pattern or any alternative patterns		
1			
2			
3			
4			
5			
6			
7			
8			

2.5: Table for analysing life values against paid work

Very important	My present job	Job alternative no. 1	job alternative no. 2
1	_ X 8 =	_X 8 =	_X 8 =
2	_ X 7 =	_X 7 =	_X 7 =
3	_ X 6 =	_X 6 =	_X 6 =
4	_ X 5 =	_X 5 =	_X 5 =
5	_ X 4 =	_X 4 =	_X 4 =
6	_ X 3 =	_X 3 =	_X 3 =
7	_ X 2 =	_X 2 =	_X 2 =
8	_ X 1 =	_X 1 =	_X 1 =
	TOTAL:	TOTAL:	TOTAL:
MY *NOT IMPORTANT* CARDS ARE:	Tick any of these if they feature in your current job or any alternative jobs		
1			
2			
3			
4			
5			
6			
7			
8			

APPENDIX 3

Transferable skills cards

People **PROMOTING CHANGE** *making things happen*	*Ideas* **DESIGNING THINGS** *designing things or events*
Data **ANALYSING** *analysing, dissecting, sorting and sifting through information or things*	*Things* **USING POWER TOOLS** *using machine tools, sewing machine, lathe power tools*
Ideas **USING SEARCH ENGINES** *knowing how to use web search engines like Google for research and to generate ideas*	*Ideas* **DRAWING/PAINTING** *conveying feelings or thoughts through drawing, painting, etc.*
People **SELLING** *selling, persuading, negotiating*	*Ideas* **ADAPTABILITY** *expecting and welcoming change, flexible*
Data **DIAGNOSING** *diagnosing, looking for the causes of problem*	*Ideas* **INSIGHT** *having insight into people's feelings or situations, using intuition*

Data

EXAMINING

examining, observing, surveying, having an eye for detail and accuracy

People

PERFORMING

performing in a group, on stage, in public, etc.

Ideas

WORKING CREATIVELY

working creatively with ideas, spaces, shapes or faces; lateral thinking

Data

ASSESSING

being able to differentiate between alternatives and options, able to assess the pros and cons

People

MOTIVATING

inspiring or energising others to achieve

People

LEADING

taking on a leadership role, providing direction, building teams

Things

REPAIRING

fixing or repairing things

Data

STRATEGIC THINKING

able to stand back, see the big picture, examine alternatives

Data

MANAGING MONEY

managing money, budgeting, organising finances

Data

MENTAL ARITHMETIC

manipulating numbers rapidly and accurately in one's head

Things

USING COMPUTERS

knowing how to word process, use spreadsheets, powerpoint,etc.

Things

BUILDING

building, constructing

Ideas

WRITING

writing creatively

Data

ORGANISING

organising, classifying information

Ideas

TIME MANAGEMENT

setting priorities, making lists, keeping appointments, working to schedules, reliable

Ideas

WORKING WITH COLOUR

working creatively with colours

People

DRAWING OUT

the ability to get people to share their feelings or ideas

People

GIVING CREDIT TO OTHERS

recognising and appreciating the achievements of others

Data

FOLLOWING INSTRUCTIONS

the ability to follow instructions, work from diagrams, blueprints or manuals

Data

CALCULATING

calculating, computing, working with numbers

Things **PRECISION** *handling things with precision*	*People* **LISTENING** *the ability to attend well to people*
Ideas **INNOVATIVE** *creating, innovating, seeing alternatives*	*People* **MAKING THE FIRST MOVE** *making first move in relationships*
Data **MEMORISING** *memorising numbers or data generally*	*Data* **REVIEWING** *able to stand back and learn from experience*
Data **SOLVING PROBLEMS** *problem-solving*	*People* **ORGANISING PEOPLE** *managing people to get tasks done*
Things **HAND–EYE CO-ORDINATION** *capable of rapid and precise hand movements directed by the eye and brain*	*Data* **TAKING INVENTORY** *able to make detailed lists of property, products, etc. and to sum up their worth*

People
HELPING OTHERS
committed to and good at doing things for others

People
NETWORKING
knowing how to make contact with people, collect ideas, coordinate action and to market oneself

People
SENSITIVITY
showing sensitivity to others' feelings

People
TEACHING
teaching, training, coaching, mentoring

Things
USING HAND TOOLS
using hand tools

Things
KEYBOARD SKILLS
using computers, mobile phones, iPods, etc.

Things
KEEPING FIT
keeping physically fit

Things
ASSEMBLING
putting things together

Ideas
DEVELOPING IDEAS
developing other's ideas

Ideas
MUSICAL
composing, playing or performing music

Ideas	*Things*
IMPROVISING	**FINDING OUT HOW THINGS WORK**
improvising, adapting	*able to analyse, take things apart and reassemble them*

Things	*Things*
PHYSICAL STRENGTH	**DRIVING**
physically strong	*driving car, motorbike*

Ideas	*Things*
CURIOSITY	**QUICK REACTIONS**
having an enquiring mind, keen to pursue new knowledge, questioning	*quick physical reactions*

VERY COMPETENT

COMPETENT

ADEQUATE

UNDEVELOPED

APPENDIX 4

Career and life planning at 50+ – a questionnaire

This was the questionnaire that was sent out, responses to which formed the basis of many of the quotations in this book. You may find it an interesting exercise to consider what your responses would have been!

Section 1: my career and life review
1. What jobs have you had since you were 50?
2. What education or training have you had since you were 50?
3. What goals or ambitions do you have for the second half of your life?
4. What have been the most rewarding experiences you have since you were 50 and what made them so?
5. What has given your career or your life stimulus or purpose since you were 50?
6. Can you remember different attitudes to career and life at different ages? If so, what were these in your 20s and 30s?
What were these in your 40s?
What were these in your 50s?
What were these in your 60s?
What were these in your 70s?

What were these in your 80s?

7. What do you see as the most significant factors which will affect career and life decisions for people of 50+, over the next 25 years?

8. What have been the most important lessons you have learned in your lifetime?

9. What do you think are the most important sources of 'quality of life' at 50+?

Section 2: work

10. How has 'the world of work' and what it offers changed in your lifetime?

11. What would you say your job(s) has/have given you over the years?

12. What experience have you had of doing unpaid work? Why did you do it and what did you learn from the experience?

13. How have things outside of jobs influenced your life and career since you turned 50? (e.g. health, relationships, economic pressures, pensions, windfalls, bereavements, etc.)

14. What are your thoughts and feelings about retirement?

15. What has been your experience of, and attitude to, work–life balance at different stages in your history? What is your approach to it now?

16. What differences do you see in the career and life planning challenges you have faced or are facing and those your parents' generation faced?

Section 3: finance

17. Has your attitude to 'money' changed over the years and if so in what way?

18. How much financial planning have you done for your future since you were 50?

19. What are the best financial planning decisions you have made and what made them good?

20. What were the worst financial planning decisions you have made and what made them so?

21. What advice would you give to anybody addressing financial planning for their future for the first time?

Section 4: health

22. In what ways have you sought to maintain or enhance your health and fitness since reaching 50?

23. How would you describe your attitude to ageing?

Section 5: learning and development

24. In what ways have you engaged with education or training since reaching 50, and what was your motivation?

25. What are your future ambitions for further learning and development?

26. How has new technology impacted on your career and your life after the age of 50 and how have you responded to that?

Section 6: relationships

27. How have close relationships affected your life and career decisions since you were 50? (E.g. spouses, partners, children, grandchildren, ageing parents?)

Section 7: spirituality

28. Would you say there has been or is a spiritual dimension to your life?

29. If so, what does spirituality mean to you and how is it important to you?

30. Have your views on spirituality changed post 50?

Section 8: leisure

31. How, if at all, has your use of leisure changed since you were 50?

32. How have hobbies or special interests contributed to the second half of your life?

Section 9: responding to the unpredictable

33. Have you experienced any unpredictable events in your life that called for major changes in your plans or directions (e.g. illnesses, health problems (yours or others), relationship breakdowns, bereavements, national or world events, financial windfalls, new relationships etc.)? If so, what were they, what impact did they have and how did you respond?

34. What advice would you give to somebody whose plans or ambitions have to be significantly re-assessed after such events?

35. Have you had any particularly special experience that has enhanced your life and/or career? If so, what did it involve and what enrichment did it provide?

Section 10: and finally...

36. What have been the most rewarding or satisfying periods of your life or career so far and what made them so?

37. What are your plans for the future?

38. Are there any final thoughts or words that you think would be valuable to those involved in reviewing their life and career or re-shaping their future?

APPENDIX 5

My 'Aha' pages

Although we would recommend a separate note book or ringbinder, which would allow you to make fuller notes, you may wish to jot odd notes or thoughts here, as you work through the book.

'Aha' Notes

'Aha' Notes

'Aha' Notes

'Aha' Notes

'Aha' Notes